CASE STUDIES IN
CULTURAL ANTHROPOLOGY

GENERAL EDITORS
George and Louise Spindler
STANFORD UNIVERSITY

LIFE IN A TURKISH VILLAGE

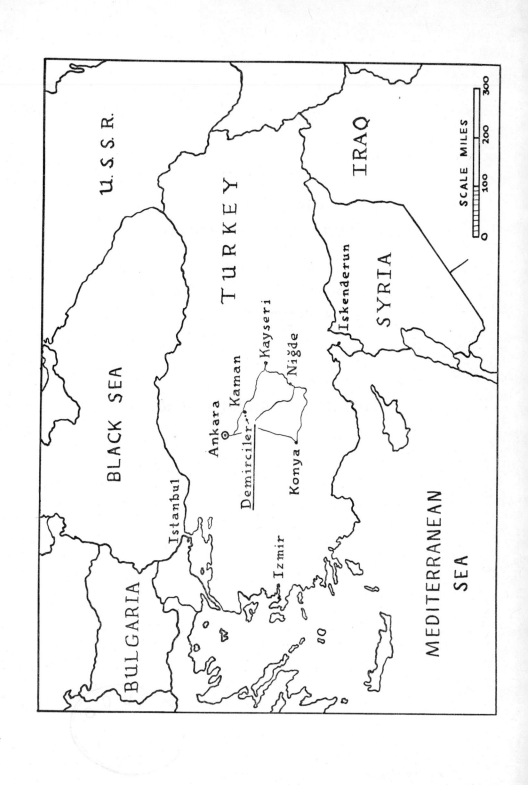

LIFE in a TURKISH VILLAGE

By

JOE E. PIERCE
Portland State College

HOLT, RINEHART AND WINSTON

NEW YORK   CHICAGO   SAN FRANCISCO   TORONTO   LONDON

Foreword

About the Series

These case studies in cultural anthropology are designed to bring to students, in beginning and intermediate courses in the social sciences, insights into the richness and complexity of human life as it is lived in different ways and in different places. They are written by men and women who have lived in societies they write about, and who are professionally trained as observers and interpreters of human behavior. The authors are also teachers, and in writing their books they have kept the students who will read them foremost in their minds. It is our belief that when an understanding of ways of life very different from one's own is gained, abstractions and generalizations about social structure, cultural values, subsistence techniques, and the other universal categories of human social behavior become meaningful.

About the Author

Joe E. Pierce is associate professor of anthropology at Portland State College. He holds the Ph.D. in anthropology from Indiana University. He has done field work with American Indians in Oklahoma (1954) and Oregon (1962–1963) in addition to six and one-half years of residence in Turkey. Major research projects include a morpheme count of Turkish and a salvage program for Indian languages of Oregon. He has written an English language textbook for the sixth grade in the Turkish public school system and a spoken English book for beginning adults who are native speakers of Turkish, as well as a handbook for teachers of second languages. He has also taught at the Political Science Faculty of Ankara University and the Gazi Teachers' Training Institute in Ankara, Turkey, while an assistant professor of linguistics at Georgetown University. He is a fellow in the American Anthropological Association, a member of the Linguistic Society of America, Sigma Xi, the American Oriental Society, and a member of the board of directors of the Portland American Indian Foundation and Center.

About the Book

This case study is divided into two parts. In the first part one sees life in an Anatolian village through the eyes of a small boy who is just beginning the long induction into a man's role. The reader experiences vividly with Mahmud a great range of activities—from building a house to learning a kinship system. These areas of behavior encountered through Mahmud's experiences are the same ones that would be covered in a conventional monograph, but they are introduced in an especially lively way through this unusual approach.

In Part Two the author shifts abruptly to a more conventional analysis of Anatolian village life. He presents straightforward descriptive interpretations of the social system, economy, political structure, religious and folk beliefs, and an intriguing chapter on language and a world view. The reader can therefore grasp both the picture of life from the inside in Part One and the more detached anthropological view of the same system in Part Two. The author concludes with a brief statement of theory applied to the problems inherent in the attempt to observe and sort out the facts of life in any community.

GEORGE AND LOUISE SPINDLER
General Editors

Stanford, California
1964

Preface

Demirciler consists of about 60 houses and in each house lives an extended family (a man and his wife, with their sons and wives, unmarried daughters, and the children of their sons). The village is located on a vast semiarid plateau near the city of Kaman, Turkey, slightly over 100 kilometers southeast of Ankara. The surrounding countryside is either tilled, mostly to wheat, or used for the grazing of herds of sheep and goats. The road between Kaman and Ankara runs past the village at a distance of between two and three kilometers at the nearest point.

Until very recently the world of the villager consisted of the valley in which he lived. Everything of value to him was in this valley. He produced almost everything he consumed and consumed nearly everything he produced. Almost everyone born in the valley lived and died there. In Demirciler he would marry someone who had also been born and reared there. Hence, such things as international politics or even national politics did not concern him much. The points at which the life of the nation impinged on his own were the required two years of military service and national taxes. Thus the world was split into two different worlds: (1) his valley, including Kaman, and (2) the outside world, including the rest of Turkey.

Within the valley around Demirciler the residents of the village felt themselves to be different from the residents of the other villages, despite the fact that they shared much the same cultural heritage, and they felt even more different from the city dwellers in Kaman. Within the village people were pictured to be of two different types: (1) superior males and (2) inferior females. The village population was further divided into: (1) old people who had prestige and honor; (2) adults, who did most of the normal day-to-day work within the community; and (3) the children, who had no authority and no responsibilities for the running of the community.

Part One of this book takes a small boy and leads him through many of the activities in the village. Mahmud, as I will name the boy, represents anyone attempting to learn about the culture. As Mahmud learns about his culture so can the reader. I felt that this method of introducing the village would give the reader a feeling for the character of village life that would be less directly communicated by the normal monographic approach. However, since the book is meant for use as a case study in anthropology courses, as well as for anyone who happens to be interested in rural Turkish life, Part Two gives a more traditional description of the culture with some comments about problems inherent in field work.

J. E. P.

Portland, Oregon
1964

Contents

Right: Old Muhtar and an elder of the village in the room for men in the old Muhtar's house.

Above: Woman and her daughter beside the fireplace in their kitchen.

Right: Two sisters from a neighboring village standing before their home.

Left: A hay rack, oxcart, and farmer.

Above: Woman and her daughter threshing grain.

Left: Man and his son demonstrating how to use pitchforks.

Introduction

THE FIELD WORK on which this report is based was carried out during six and one-half years of residence in Turkey. Innumerable trips were made to villages throughout the country, but since my home was in Ankara, the Anatolian villages were more accessible than those in the east or along the coast.

In one sense this book describes a composite village, drawn from my observations in several villages. In another sense it is a book about one village. During my residence in Ankara I was most fortunate in obtaining the services of an informant, a young man, who worked with me for about two years whenever my job permitted. The detailed picture of life in his village, which was secured through these informative sessions, gave me a view of the culture in depth that I would otherwise have lacked. In a visit to his village I was able to check my own observations against his, and his mother supplied valuable additional information. The details of life in one Anatolian village secured from these two people are given a broad context by observations in the other villages that I visited.

The data were not collected with any particular theoretical problem in mind. My only desire was to learn as much about Anatolian villages as I could in order to bring the information back for the benefit of my students in the United States. I have tried to present as simply and accurately as possible a picture of the life of a peasant in such a village. Because the very collection of data must be based on some set of assumptions, I have included some statements on theoretical orientation in the second part of the book. My hope is that I have presented the culture in terms of the functionally significant categories for Turkish society and not in terms of preconceived Western categories.

PART ONE

Mahmud's Village

$$\boxed{\text{I}}$$

The Circumcision

OUTSIDE, the bright Anatolian sky was filled with sunshine, as it had been on many days before this one, but today Mahmud was frightened. The familiar objects of his life were still around the room, yet they did not relieve his fears. In a corner he could see the little wire wagon that he had been pulling about the village streets a few days before. His father stood beside the bed glancing nervously toward the door, and some of the men talked and joked with him as noises of the other villagers, obviously enjoying the day, drifted in through the open window. The walls seemed to be a much brighter white than usual, and every object was cleaned and standing properly in its place, but this day was different. For this was the day of his circumcision party.

Many things had led up to this day. Mahmud's parents had told him repeatedly and with great joy that it would soon be time for his *Sünnet Düğünü* This had meant little to him at first, but when he proudly announced it to his playmates, the older boys had teased him in a way that made him wonder what it was all about. When he had finally asked them, each had told the story of his own Sünnet, embellished as best the narrator could to make it the more frightening.

Mahmud had run home to tell his father, who had scoffed at the idea that it was a terrible thing and reassured him that it was really nothing. Besides, his father had added, "It is the commandment of Allah," and that had ended any discussion of the matter, as it always did, for one was not permitted to question the will of Allah. To Mahmud this merely made the circumcision seem to be something supernatural and even more to be feared.

For the past few days he had watched with a mixture of pleasure and anxiety as relatives and friends brought sheep, chickens, and vegetables for the coming feast. The day before all the women in his family, along with many aunts and cousins, had begun to prepare the food that would feed the entire village. Throughout all of these preparations people came over to congratulate him or make remarks about his growing up, and he was pleased to be the center of so

4

much attention, but between these periods of pleasure, when all was quiet and no one concerned themselves with him, Mahmud felt nervous and fearful.

Early that morning he had been dressed in a new white dress, trimmed with strips of red cloth, and a flat circular blue hat, decorated with threads of pure gold, had been fixed securely to his head. Shortly after breakfast a drummer and flute player had struck up their familiar music, and the men began to gather in the *Muhtar's* (village headman) home, but Mahmud had been told only that this was the day.

The morning had passed quite normally as children ran about the village and chased sheep, dogs, or each other. Then at noon there had been much to eat for all. Shortly after that his father had taken him by the hand and they had joined the other men at the Muhtar's home. There the musicians were playing and some of the villagers were dancing. The time had passed quickly, sitting in the men's room; at midafternoon he had been taken outside where a horse stood waiting for him. This was not just an ordinary ride on a horse, however, for the animal was decorated with strips of gayly colored cloth and carried a new saddle on its back. On this mount he had been led by his father around the village and up and down all of the streets until finally they had come to Mahmud's home.

Relieved somewhat by the memories of a very pleasant day, Mahmud relaxed a little, but the click of the door startled his still somewhat tense body as the *Sünnetci,* who would perform the operation, entered the room smiling. Greeting Mahmud pleasantly, he spoke soothingly to the boy, and then went to shake hands with his father and the other men.

Coming to the bedside the Sünnetci sat down and began to tease the boy, hiding a small sharp knife in the cupped palm of his right hand. Soon the fears were gone, and Mahmud was laughing with a man whom he had seen about the village all his life. As if it were nothing at all, the man suddenly caught the end of Mahmud's penis with one hand and with a quick stroke severed the foreskin, and the sharp pain brough tears momentarily to Mahmud's eyes. However, before he could really begin to cry, he was in his father's arms and the voice of a proud parent was telling him what a good boy he had been not to cry, and naturally he had to stifle the tears.

After a few seconds his father put him back on the bed, and the Sünnetci powdered the injured organ before the men came over to congratulate him again. Many of them told him how brave he had been, and before long the pain of it all was forgotten.

The bed was pulled near the open window, and pillows were placed behind his back so that he could sit up and look out at the dancers. By this time the flute was whining incessantly, and Mahmud watched the flutist who never let his music stop. It seemed that the man would have to breathe sometime, but Mahmud had not figured out how, for the music whined on and on without a single interruption. The drummer nearby thumped out two different rhythms, one on either side of the instrument. In his right hand the man held a large stick with a rounded head on it with which he pounded out a fairly steady beat, but in his left hand he held two thin sticks that moved more rapidly, making an uneven rhythm. In a large empty space near the house a long row of men were holding hands and kicking up the dry dust of the village street with their feet as they shouted and moved quickly about following the leadership of a man on one end of the line who waved a handkerchief.

Shortly after the completion of the cutting itself, members of Mahmud's family began to come in singly and in small groups to wish him well, to give presents, or just to say *Maṣallah,* but even being the center of attention became wearisome after a while and he looked out the window again. The streets were filled with men and boys, but all the women sat on the rooftops to watch the activity.

Since his father's house was to the east of the village proper and situated on a rather steep rise, he could see all of the 60 or so houses that made up the settlement. Far to the left and down near the foot of the hill was the village fountain. It was a native stone structure, held together by concrete, with four steel pipes spouting water steadily in small streams. Usually there would be girls there washing clothes or dishes, but today only a lone child collected water in a copper container. The girl was only a little older than Mahmud, and he wondered what she had been doing and who she was getting the water for.

These were but fleeting ideas in a meandering mind, however, as far to the west a cloud of dust caught his eye, and he knew it must be a car on the highway to Ankara. He wondered momentarily what Ankara was. It was really only a name to him, and the thought vanished as did the dust cloud when the car disappeared in the distance.

Looking about in every direction, he could see a long way toward the west, where the rolling hills gradually grew in height. Here and there the uncultivated land was spotted by a small patch of trees, and even a boy as young as Mahmud knew that there were springs beneath the foliage, for the rainfall here was so scarce that trees could not grow uncared for in the open.

Not far to the right he could see the tile rooftops of the provincial capital, in reality a small city, but very large in the eyes of a little boy who had been raised in the village. It was not far away, but he had rarely been there. Next year he would go to school, and his parents had told him that he would have to walk there and back every day. This seemed unbelievable, but what his parents said was usually true so this thought too passed from his mind.

Looking to the left again, his eyes followed the narrow village street, unpaved and very rough, but good enough for man and sheep to walk on. Few cars came to the village so there was no need for better roads.

The flat-roofed, mud-brick homes of his friends and relatives were scattered helter-skelter as if someone had dropped them from the sky and left them where they had landed. Most were single-story houses with a cylindrical stone roller resting on the roof near the chimney. This implement was used to repack the mud roof each spring after the winter rains. Going inside any of these houses, one entered first a hallway about six feet wide and six feet long. On the right was the men's living room, a squarish compartment about 12 by 12 feet, the largest and finest in the house. The furniture in this room consisted of a long, low sofalike structure projecting about half a yard from the wall opposite the entryway and extending across the room. A few of the houses had, in addition, a bed that was a tablelike platform, also built out from the wall, and a couple of plain wooden chairs, purchased in the nearby city. These latter items were, however, very expensive, and only the wealthy villagers could afford them. The floors were carpeted with brightly colored rugs, woven in the village, and small tapestries, also locally made, decorated the walls and sofa. Pillows were covered with beautifully embroidered designs, sometimes incorporating threads of pure silver. In the houses without chairs or beds the inhabitants sat and slept on the floors.

Across the hall, on the left as you entered, was the women's living room, which was almost identical to that of the men, but somewhat smaller and less elaborately furnished. At the end of the hallway were two doors. The one on the left opened into a toilet, which was a concrete floor with a funnel-shaped opening disappearing into the earth. On either side and slightly to the front of this hole were two concrete footprints, and near at hand was the familiar copper water container that was used for ablutions after defecation and for flushing the toilet as well. Adjoining this room was another similar one which was furnished only with a tin container suspended from the wall about waist high, with a small faucet at the bottom. On top of this rested a mirror and a bottle of lemon cologne. Each morning the young girls filled this container from the fountain, and everyone washed in running water that fell to the floor and went out of the house through a small hole in the wall onto the rocky ground to be evaporated by the hot sun. Just outside the door was a row of wooden pegs from which hung clean turkish towels on which both the family and guests dried themselves. The government had promised to pipe water into their houses by 1962.

Facing these two small rooms, one could turn to the left and see the kitchen, a long hall-like compartment about four feet wide and twelve feet long with a fireplace on one wall. A small waist-high projection that looked like a table ran the length of the room just beneath the fireplace.

Turning to the right one could see another small room—this one was used mostly for storage, but sometimes it served to sleep guests. Here again was the sofalike projection similar to those in the men's and women's rooms. Every house in the village was built along this same plan, but some were small, others large, and in each lived a man, his wife and children, and their wives and children. Single-storied houses usually had an additional room for the animals, and two-storied houses utilized the ground floor for storage and the animals.

Inside all but a few of these houses the walls were brilliantly clean with whitewash, which was applied by the villagers every two or three years as needed. The windows were about a yard square and framed with unpainted wood. The floors and doors were also unpainted, as paint was extremely expensive. Most rooms were lighted with an electric bulb of about 50 watts, hanging by a single-strand wire from the ceiling, (electricity having been brought to the village in 1958). Mahmud could remember that when he had been very small the poorer villagers had lighted their homes with kerosene and the wealthier ones with gasoline lanterns, but things were improving rapidly. The Muhtar now had a rough wooden European-type table in his hallway to eat on, though the villagers almost always ate on small portable tables that reached up just over a foot from the floor. Nearly all of the homes had at least one small single-burner kerosene stove and the fireplaces were rarely used for cooking, except when the families ran low on money or when more than one fire was needed at a time. In cold weather a good charcoal fire provided much more economical heating than did kerosene, so the fireplace retained at least some of its importance, though only secondarily for cooking.

As Mahmud thought about these things, the pictures gradually grew dimmer and finally faded away completely, along with the noises from the street, and soon he was fast asleep. His mother came in and tucked the covers around him, smiled at his face for a long time, then whispered a brief prayer of thanks to Allah for such a fine healthy boy, asked for a long and good life for this her son, and left him alone to sleep undisturbed through the night.

2

The Building of a House

THE NEXT MORNING Mahmud remembered only the pleasures of the feasting, the special ride about the village on the horse, and the gifts, so he bounced out of bed as he always did and felt only that he had in some way grown a little older. His mother took one of the large circles of unleavened village bread, which was less than an eighth of an inch thick and about 18 inches in diameter, tore a large piece off it, and gave this to him with a piece of *prassı*, a vegetable which looks like a green onion but which grows to about 30 inches in length with a diameter of a little over one inch. Grabbing the proffered food, he ran out into the yard, eating as he went. This was his breakfast.

Going nowhere in particular, he ambled aimlessly about the streets for some time before stopping to watch one of the old women spinning the yarn with which she would weave a heavy woolen vest for someone in her family or perhaps a small rug. Though he had seen this activity many times before, Mahmud never tired of watching the small puffs of raw sheep's wool gradually turn into course thread as the woman fed it evenly out from her right hand. The lower ends of the fibers were fastened to a small wooden shaft that was enlarged near the top. As she let the wool out carefully, she kept the spindle whorl swinging slowly back and forth, and each time it passed her body, the enlarged portion would strike her thigh. This action imparted a spinning motion to the whorl. The weight of the wooden shaft applied just the right amount of pressure to form good thread if the old woman was careful to feed out just the right amount of wool. Many years ago all of their clothing had been made from this yarn, or at least so Mahmud had been told, but now most of their everyday clothes were made from cotton cloth bought in town.

The old woman was wearing three pairs of billowing pantaloons, one on top the other, all of which were made of brightly colored cotton flannel prints. These, pantaloons typical of most Anatolian villages, were very loose, and were sewn together at the bottom only a few inches above the ground, fitting tight about the ankles, and being drawn about the waist by a drawstring.

The woman's upper body was covered by a blouse, also loosely made, but tight at the wrists and neck and tucked into the pantaloons. Over this blouse she wore a heavy sleeveless vest woven from the thread that she was spinning. Over the pantaloons she wore a skirt, made of brightly colored cloth of a different pattern and color, that was tied tightly about the waist and hung down to about halfway between the knees and ankles. Her head was covered with a *çarşaf* (scarf) that exposed no hair but left the face uncovered, for Atatürk had suggested that women need no longer go about veiled as had been required by Moslem law in the past. Now her face was covered only in the presence of strange men, and sometimes not even then.

Mahmud was still interested in the intricate work of making thread, but not far away he could hear the noises of men mixing earth with water to prepare the mud bricks from which the village houses were made. Gradually the desire to be with those of his own sex and share in what he considered to be men's work drew his attention from the old woman, and he made his way slowly toward the southeast where a small group of men were mixing earth, water, and hay to form the bricks for a new house.

"*Büyük Babacim* (my dear grandfather) how do you know how much water to put in it?" Mahmud asked one of the old men as he came up.

"He just knows," a bystander answered.

"How?" Mahmud repeated his question.

"He is the *Usta*," the man shrugged, and Mahmud knew that *usta* meant master or expert, and that no further explanation would be forthcoming, though it did not answer his question.

Lapsing into silence, the boy watched some hay being stirred into the mud and more water being added until the old man said that it was *tamam*. Then the building material was put into molds about four inches wide, four inches deep, and eight inches long. Many of these molds were needed, as the building blocks had to remain in them overnight before they were dumped out of the molds and left on the ground to be dried by the hot Anatolian sun. Some bricks that had been made over a week before were now sufficiently dry, and a group of the older boys were gathering them together, carrying them to a spot near where the walls of a new house were being made and stacking them there in a neat pile.

Someone called to Mahmud, "You're no longer a baby, so get to work," and he ran quickly to help carry the bricks.

Two men about the age of Mahmud's father were building the walls higher by first covering a portion of the upper surface with a thin layer of the same material from which the bricks were being made and then laying four bricks parallel with the length of the wall across it. More of the soft mudlike mixture was placed between the bricks to act as mortar, and when these were firmly in place, two more were set end to end across the wall and mortared tightly against the ends of the blocks already in position. Then a second pair of bricks were aligned in the same manner before another row of four were cemented across the wall. Thus Mahmud watched the house go up as he carried the dried bricks.

The building progressed quite rapidly, and only a few days later, when Mahmud was again helping with the work, the wall reached its desired height, and an older man brought a load of poles from a nearby grove to support the roof. These were poplar trunks, grown specially for this purpose, with the bark stripped off. Slowly the old man got off his wagon, which seemed very long to Mahmud. It was actually about 45 feet in length, but then it was not really a single vehicle. It did have two pairs of wheels, one in front and one in back, but they were not connected, and when the logs were removed, the rear wheels were completely free from the front ones, which were harnessed to a team of yoked oxen.

The old man untied the thin poles and several of the youngsters ran to help unload, but Mahmud did not try this. The logs were heavy and he could be badly hurt if one of them fell on him, so he left this dangerous activity to the older boys.

The oxen stood idly chewing their cud as Mahmud examined the large wheels of solid wood that were bound tightly together by a steel band around the outer edge. The square axle, protruding through the wooden disks, was held in place by a wedge-shaped peg, also of wood. The frame itself consisted of nothing more than two large logs, squared roughly to about eight inches with a crude hand axe. The wheels did not turn on the axle, but rather the entire assembly, which formed a solid unit, turned together beneath the frame of the wagon.

Protruding from the upper structure and extending from front to back beneath the vehicle was a straight pole about six feet in length to which the logs had been lashed. The tongue was attached firmly to the frame and reached up to the necks of the oxen where it was secured tightly to the wooden yoke that was carved to fit over the oxen's humps. Beneath the necks of the animals was another piece of wood, pulled up tightly so that it would not rub sores on the oxen. This yoke enabled the animals to drag fairly heavy loads with only slight discomfort.

As Mahmud had been engrossed in examining the engineering of the wagon, the old man had finished his supervision of the unloading process and started toward the building. Seeing the boy, he paused, came over to where Mahmud was standing, ruffled his hair, and growled, almost unpleasantly, "So you had your Sünnet, did you? Well now, maybe we can get some work out of you."

Even this gruff message from an old man impressed upon Mahmud the fact that he was growing up and filled him with a warm, pleasant pride in himself. Knowing of no answer, the boy only grinned sheepishly and said nothing. However, the old man understood very well what boys thought, for he had been one himself, and so he walked away, still looking very gruff, but remembering the pleasures of being a boy.

Watching the man walk away, Mahmud remembered playing in the poplar grove near the large spring which was about a mile from his home. This belonged to the Muhtar, but the old man who had brought the timbers watched over it, cut the trees when they were ready, and delivered them to the people in the village when they were needed.

The poplar grove was an interesting place, for trees did not grow uncared for in central Anatolia. They must be planted each year and watched over carefully to keep them from being eaten by the sheep and goats or dying from lack of water. The grove was divided into patches, and one area planted each year. These trees grew about ten feet in a season and therefore the various patches were easily distinguishable by their differences in height. The old man's job was not an easy one, for the trees had to be very carefully spaced and lined up so that no land was wasted. If the trees were set too close together many would die.

When people from the village ordered trees for the roofs of their houses, the old man had to cut them down without destroying any of the others, strip the bark from the trunks, and deliver them to their buyers. The logs had arrived this morning, because the new home-owner had said that the walls would be high enough to start putting on the roof by today, and the old man was always on time. On time meant something quite different to him, however, from what it meant to the people in the city. When he said that he would bring the logs in the morning, this meant before the time for midday prayers, nothing more. He might appear shortly after sunrise or just before noon. He would never promise for a more specific time than that, because his life was regulated by the five prayers that Moslem law required him to make each day, and he never missed one of them. These broke the daylight hours up into four segments that were quite accurate enough for the people in the village. The old man prayed religiously at sunrise, midmorning, noon, midafternoon, and sunset every day, and these prayers gave meaning to his life and peace to his soul, besides providing a method of measuring the time.

When the old man reached the walls of the new house, the poles were being lifted to the top by the older boys to form the base for the roof. Several hours passed as these were fitted in place and turned slightly this way or that so as to form the flattest possible surface. Each log was then cemented to the wall with more of the mudlike mortar so that the logs were evenly spaced at about 15 inches apart. Then mats, woven from cane leaves, were laid across these beams, making a solid surface. Large masses of dry poplar leaves were then laid in place to form the base for the roof covering that was made of the same material as the bricks, except that it had been thinned by the addition of a little extra water. A heavy layer of this mixture was applied over the leaves, then smoothed by hand, allowed to dry for a day or so, and finally rolled out very hard with a heavy cylinderical stone, which then remained atop the building for repacking the surface whenever it might be needed.

As the roof was being pressed and smoothed, other men were plastering the recently completed walls with a heavy layer of the same mixture of earth, water, and straw. The window frames were being set in place at the same time, and the hard-packed earth floor was being covered with the mortarlike substance. After all this was completed a man would be called from the city to come and spray a mixture of white earth and water over the interior walls, and the new home would be completed.

New buildings were not constructed often in the village, though many more were being built now then had been the case in years past. With the coming of modern doctors to the city nearby, fewer babies died and a village population that had been nearly stable for as long as anyone knew had more than doubled in the past ten years. In the old days a woman who had eight or ten children considered herself lucky if three or four of them grew to maturity, so new homes were not often needed.

The owner of this house was one of Mahmud's uncles, who had been married for several years and was just now getting around to building one of his own. He and his wife and children had lived with his father to the present time, but the old man had died recently, and the house had gone to his older brother, so he decided that it would be good to have a home of his own.

3

A Marriage

A S THE WEEKS and months went by Mahmud grew older and entered school, just as his parents had said that he would. Each morning he walked the two kilometers to the city in company with the other school-age children, taking half a loaf of bread and some fruit for lunch, and returned in the evening. School life was very different from that in the village, but when he was at home things went on pretty much as they always had.

Even in the village, however, things new to Mahmud happened occasionally, and one evening he heard his father and mother talking softly in the hallway between the two living rooms. They were whispering so that no one could understand what they were saying, but this only made him want more than ever to hear, and so he edged nearer to where they were standing and listened intently, in the shadows near the doorway. The conversation concerned his older sister who was nearly sixteen and old enough to be married.

"What will you tell them?" his mother said.

"I don't know just yet," his father answered.

"But they will come tomorrow, and you know that they have been here twice already. They will want to know tomorrow, and you cannot wait until then to decide," the wife insisted.

This reminded Mahmud of the two special visits in recent weeks by the mother and father of one of his friends who lived just down the street. He had not understood their purpose then, but the family had come to look over his sister as a prospective wife for their son who would soon be old enough to go into the army and should be married before he left. Thinking back on the visits, Mahmud remembered how his sister had each time been told well in advance that they were coming and that she had spent hours getting dressed, preparing fruits and nuts for the visitors, and asking her mother if she should do this or that when they arrived.

At the very first knock she ran to the door. As they came in, she kissed first the back of the hand of the man and lifted it to her forehead, then did the

14

same to the woman. Mahmud's mother and father had also welcomed the guests. Then the men had gone into the men's room and the women into the women's. As they sat talking, the visitors would call in and ask for this or that, and Mahmud's sister would run to bring what they asked for as quickly as she could. On the second visit the mother had asked her to make some coffee, and she had very carefully and skillfully demonstrated her ability to handle cooking utensils. They had seemed pleased, and his sister appeared to be happy, but he did not quite understand it all.

Now it became clear, as he listened to the talk of his mother and father. The visitors had thought his sister would make a good wife for their son or they would not have come back again. Now that they were coming a third time, it meant that they might very well ask for a final decision about the arrangements. If they were not completely satisfied, they might come once more, but Mahmud's mother felt that they should have an answer ready before tomorrow, just in case the boy's parents did want to settle it all then.

The prospective husband was of a good family. He was quite nice looking, a hard worker, and the daughter liked him, from a distance of course, as she was not allowed to talk with boys his age. There seemed to be no obvious reason for not accepting, but Mahmud's father was worried about how much money the family would give. He realized that his daughter was an unusually pretty girl and that this was only the first family to ask. He wondered if they should accept if the man offered them 5000 lira, bargain for more, or just wait for a better offer, but Mahmud's mother said that almost any girl in the village was worth that much, and Fatma should be worth much more.

This was not a sale of their daughter, because all the money would be used to buy furniture for the couple after they were married and to pay for the wedding feast. Still, the more they could get, the better their daughter would be able to outfit her household. After much discussion it was decided that they would not accept less than 6000 lira, but that would be a fair amount considering that Fatma would go into a fine family and, after all, she was getting an exceptional husband out of the deal too.

After having settled this problem they turned the conversation to that of finding a bride for their oldest son, who was also nearing military age and should be married before he was called away. Ali had come to his father just a few days before and said that he would like to have a marriage arranged with a certain girl who lived nearby. Actually, no one was permitted to marry outside the village, but since Ayşe was a local girl this presented no problem. The first thing that Mahmud's father had to do was trace the relationship between his son and the girl. This was necessary because she had to be at least seven steps (degrees of relationship) away. She was the daughter of the grandson of Ali's great grandfather's brother. Therefore, she would be exactly seven steps away, and the marriage would be all right. Mahmud's brother was one step from his father, two from his father's father, three steps from his great grandfather, four steps from his father's grandfather's brother, five steps from his great grandfather's brother's son, six steps from his son, and seven steps away from the son's daughter. Once this detail had been settled, only one question remained—was the family a good one? Apparently they felt that it was, as plans were bing made to ask one of Mahmud's uncles to go alone on the first visit to feel out the parents and see if they were generally in favor of such a marriage or not. If not, then the family could withdraw without any ill feelings. If they appeared to be favorable to such a union, then Mahmud's parents would go later, along with the uncle or alone, to look the girl over carefully.

Mahmud wondered why no one in the village ever married people from the city, or other villages, but he knew that for some reason this was forbidden.[1] Someone said that there was a village somewhere, where the people were also their relatives, to which young people could go to marry, but he had never known of anyone who had done it. He wondered also if there really were such a place, and if so where it was, but these things he did not know.

Soon he got ready for bed and slept soundly, without a thought about the conversations that he had overheard. Early next morning he rose and had hot tea, bread, and white cheese for breakfast. After eating he went out in the yard to play with the other children. In the afternoon he hung around the house waiting for the parents of the boy who wanted to marry his sister. Late in the day a knock was heard on the door sounding their arrival. Again he watched as his sister went to the door, kissed the hands of the visitors respectfully, and jumped to serve their every wish. Finally, after a rather long visit, the man asked Mahmud's father what he thought of arranging a marriage between the two young people. He had been cautious, approving with some hesitancy, until the man offered 7000 lira in payment to cover the wedding costs. With the amount proffered it would have been almost impossible for anyone not to enter wholeheartedly into the agreement, and it was settled that within a few weeks the couple would be married.

The next few days were very confused for Mahmud, as his mother and father, sometimes with his sister and sometimes alone, made many trips to the city to buy things for the new household with the money provided by the boy's parents. At first the things just accumulated in the house, then one day Mahmud's parents took a great deal of them on donkeys to the house of the boy's parents, where their daughter would go to set up her new home. There the old people arranged a room for the new couple, not consulting the young people at all. A great many things remained in the home of the bride, to be taken on the wedding day, but most of the larger items of furniture were moved early.

---

[1] Demirciler is endogamous (cf. Chapter XVI), but most of the other Turkish villages with which I am familiar are not. However, one could not tell this village from any other without a detailed study of the social structure. Houses, subsistence patterns, clothing, and so on appear to be typical of the area. At least one item of folklore found in Demirciler, the tale of the three brothers who separated and founded different villages, occurs among some Kurdish groups (Indo-European speaking tribes in Eastern Turkey and adjacent areas who are culturally quite distinct from Turks). Thus Demirciler may be a highly acculturated Kurdish village, but none of the people were aware of being anything but Turkish, and I found no obvious traces of Kurdish in the language, though there may be some. Anatolia is a particularly interesting place to work, as the variety of villages is almost endless. Throughout the centuries one conqueror after another has ruled the area, and each invading group has left its imprint on the villages. While each village presents an over-all appearance of similiarity, one finds some elements of the culture in each village that do not exist in others.

Then one day Mahmud was told that the *nişan* (engagement) would be very soon, and his mother and the other women in the family began to prepare food for the party. A large quantity of *pilaf* (rice), lamb, vegetables, and many other things were gathered together and made ready to be cooked. Finally, the day arrived, and the boy came with his parents to Mahmud's home. The small six-legged stand was set up in the men's room, and a large copper tray placed on top of it. The men sat around this on the floor, and the women prepared the food in the kitchen and brought it out, handed it to one of the young boys who brought it into the men's room and set it on the tray. The men ate what they wanted, and the dishes were removed and replaced with others until all had eaten their fill. Then, and only then, the women and children ate in the kitchen while the men discussed the coming marriage. Late in the evening the young people exchanged rings, and they were officially engaged.

Soon after this something happened that Mahmud could have no part in. His parents, the young couple, and the boy's mother and father went to the mosque where the *Hoca* (priest) said a long prayer in Arabic to the young people, which no one understood except the Hoca. Then he said another prayer in Turkish. This one asked God to bless the new home and give them a long and good life together. After this was over, the small group, accompanied by a few close friends of the family, went into the city where they filled out a number of papers and signed the marriage books for the government.

So far as the legal system was concerned, the couple was married, but this was not all there was to it, at least not so far as the villagers were concerned. The couple went back to the village, and each went his own way, as if nothing in particular had happened. Nearly a month later Mahmud's mother gathered together a great quantity of food, and the mother of the husband-to-be with all the women in both families came over to Mahmud's house. This group began again the preparation of large quantities of food, but this time the amount and variety were much greater than before. This was for the *düğün* (wedding), and there must be an abundance of food for the entire village for about a week.

Soon all of the money provided by the boy's parents was gone, and Mahmud's father used all of his meager savings and began to go about borrowing from his friends and relatives. Great amounts of all kinds of foods were gathered and prepared so that all that needed to be done was to cook them.

On an appointed day no one went to his fields, but a great many of the women of the village gathered at Mahmud's home, and the morning was spent placing every available table along the road in front of the house and trying to find enough pots and pans to cook in. At the same time the men all gathered in an open field on the edge of the small community where three bands, each consisting of one drummer and one flute player, had been hired to play. One of the bands was always playing, and the men danced Turkish folk dances until noon. Shortly after the midday call to prayer had been heard, they all went to the tables in front of Mahmud's house where the women served them. When the men had had all they wanted to eat, they went back to the field to dance some more, tell stories, and joke about the wedding night of the young people. Then the women ate what they wanted of what was left and spent much of the afternoon preparing for the evening meal and gossiping.

The afternoon and evening were passed in much the same manner as the morning had been. Some of the less restrained men did a little drinking, but this was frowned upon very strongly by the villagers, so few drank. In the evening everyone again ate his fill, and the dancing and merrymaking went on into the night until there was no one awake except the musicians and, finally, even they took some time off for sleep.

Five days were passed in singing, dancing, and story-telling, with no one doing any work, except the women and girls who had to feed the village, until the day on which the marriage was to be consummated finally arrived. Most of the morning was very confusing to Mahmud, as his home was filled with a continuous procession of women and children who came to see his sister and the things that she would take with her to her new home. The bride was dressed in a billowy blue and yellow pajamalike outfit made of silk and decorated with embroidery sewn with threads of pure silver, which was tight only at the wrists, ankles, and neck, and which was sewn together just a few inches above the floor. Over this she wore a dress designed like a nightshirt, which was made of red velvet, also decorated with silver embroidery, and drawn in at the waist by a belt made of silver wire. Her hair had been braided into about eight long pigtails, and in these were carefully woven strands of silver foil that were supposed to give the bride a long and happy life. Her hands up to a little above the wrists were made red with henna dye.

Mahmud's sister stood near the door and kissed the back of the hand of each visitor and raised the hand to touch her forehead. This gesture of respect was second nature for all village children even at Mahmud's age. Then his sister led the guests to view the chests in which were over 30 pairs of white socks, more than 200 scarfs, as well as a lot of towels, underclothing, dresses, pillows, and comforters. Finally, she led them to a huge pile of mattresses that stood near the back wall. These latter items were of the utmost importance for any Turkish home to be properly hospitable.

When Mahmud tired of this procession of friends and well-wishers, he went over to the home of the groom's father, where he was able to see the room that the couple would make their new home. A huge pile of copper pots and pans coated on the inside with tin, many more pillows, towels, other household items, and some very large copper wash tubs were on display along with a collection of pitchers. There were not so many people here. The women of the family were preparing the room for the coming of the bride, and visitors were dropping by to look at the furnishings, but the men were still dancing, singing, and telling stories at the edge of the village, as they had little interest in this sort of thing. Only the women, girls, and smaller boys were to be seen at either of the two houses.

Finally, the time for the noonday meal came, and Mahmud was given a bowl of *pekmez* (a grape syrup) and a large piece of bread and was told in effect that he was to stay out from under foot while the work was being done. Eating as quickly as he could, he pushed aside the dishes, decided that he would rather go out to the field and watch the dancing and listen to the older men, even though some of them did tease him a lot.

Out in the open, under the hot afternoon sky, Mahmud watched the dancing and listened to the music until just past time for the midafternoon prayer. Then the groom was brought out, the music stopped, and a large tray of very small brown berries was passed to all of the men as the father put a new suit of clothes on the young man and made the announcement that he had given his son a particular field to till and a thousand lira. Then it was time to go and get the bride, so the group split into two groups. Every man got his hunting gun and went either to the house of the bride or the house of the groom, depending on who was more closely related to him.

Mahmud's brothers and cousins knocked on the door, and his mother brought his sister out, who was covered with a bright red sheet. On her head they had first put a flat round hat, then the brilliant red bridal gown had been draped over her. She was lifted onto a waiting horse and led by her father toward her new home. The groom and his relatives had gone on ahead and were waiting on the roof of his father's house. When they saw the entourage approaching, all began to fire their rifles into the air. Mahmud's relatives answered the shots, and the bride reached her new home amid a great tumult. The new husband lifted her from the horse and took her into the room prepared for her. Still veiled, she was left there. The men then went back to their dancing, taking the husband with them, so that he could not see his new bride immediately. She remained in her new home until very late that night, when the groom was finally permitted to join her, and the marriage was consummated.

The next few weeks were even more confused for Mahmud than the ones before had been, for there was all the activity necessary for cleaning up after the great feast and so his father and mother were very busy. His father was trying to pay back as much of the money that he had borrowed as quickly as possible, because he knew that soon he would have to go through the same thing again for Mahmud's brother. Mahmud was therefore left alone by almost everyone. He was too young to do anything, and his sister's leaving had left a vacancy in the household. His sister had taken care of him when he had been very small, and it had been his habit to run to her whenever the world got to be too much for him. Now there was no one for him to turn to, and he felt very sad and walked alone a lot on the hills about the village.

4

Learning To Be a Man

THE REMAINDER of summer passed and Mahmud stayed indoors more and more, as the houses, though unheated, were warmer than the cool fall air. As the winter came and the snow fell over the countryside, most of the outdoor activities of the village ceased. The days grew shorter, the wind colder, and the snow piled high around the village. On these cold nights it was the custom for all the men to come together in the Muhtar's house, and Mahmud looked forward to these evenings with a great deal of pleasure.

Each day, after having finished the evening meal, the old Muhtar's wife would put some small earthenware dishes or copper trays filled with nuts or chick-peas about the room, sometimes on small stands or sometimes on the floor, and the old man would build a warm fire in the fireplace. Soon after dark the men would begin to arrive by ones or twos and take their accustomed places in the men's room. This was the largest single room in the village and doubled as a guest house for visitors who came at nightfall and needed some place to sleep before going on their way the next day. It had been a long time since the room had been used for this purpose, however, because the nearby growing city had hotels, and most of the modern travelers stayed there. However, the room still served as a clearing house for all village business, as well as a place for the men to pass the cold winter evenings in warm comfort.

The room was perhaps 30 by 15 feet in size, and along one side a shelf nearly 15 inches above the floor extended about 2 feet from the wall and covered the full 30 feet of the room's length. The old Muhtar sat near the center of the shelf, waiting for his guests to arrive. As the men came in, the oldest in the village would seat themselves in order of age on this raised projection, while the younger ones would sit cross-legged on the floor. No women were ever allowed to come into this room when the men were there. The Muhtar's wife had prepared everything ahead of time, and when additional things were occasionally needed during the evening, one of the boys would be sent out to fetch it. Opposite the long bench was a fireplace, slightly larger than those in the kitchens of the other village homes, in which a fire burned brightly spreading heat throughout the room. The single electric bulb lighted the space dimly and so the shadows caused by the firelight were not prevented from dancing about the walls.

Mahmud would have been happier if the electric bulb had not been there at all, the way it used to be when he had been a very small boy. Electricity had been introduced to the village only a year ago, and he remembered the days when only the glow of the fire lighted these meetings.

As the gathering grew in size, Mahmud heard many small groups of men talking idly about all sorts of personal problems, but when nearly all of the villagers had arrived, they began to quiet down.

The Hoca posed the first question, "Muhtar Bey, when will next year's money for the mosque be taken up?"

"Hocam, the amount has not been set yet," was the Muhtar's reply.

"All right, let's do it now," the Hoca persisted.

"Let's do it now," the Muhtar agreed.

And Mahmud listened as the Hoca told about the things the mosque would need during the coming year. Then several of the older men told how they had given so much the year before that it had been hard on their families, and finally, the Muhtar talked interminably about the duty of each Moslem to support the Faith and ended by asking the head of each family for just a little more than he knew they could pay.

Following this request there were a series of discussions between the Muhtar and each family head, haggling over what the members of his family could afford to give. Finally, however, agreement was reached with each man, and the Hoca knew how much he could count on for the coming year. The Muhtar would see that the money was collected and turned over to the Hoca.

The business of the evening being out of the way, Mahmud became more interested, as he knew that he liked most what was to come now. He had learned that he was too young to speak at the meetings, because he had been taken out several times the year before by one of the older boys and told that he could not stay with the men unless he could be quiet, so he waited in silence for what would happen next. After a slight pause one of the braver of the teen-aged boys called to an old man.

"*Dedem*, tell us some stories about the olden times."

"Shall I tell about the wars?" the old man nearest the Muhtar asked.

"Yes, about the great war with the Russians," the youth answered.

"Well, I was but a boy then, but my father went with the army of the Sultan that summer, and he told me this story."

It was a great army, with the generals in front on horseback and all the men, thousands of men, walking behind. They left our village in the early spring, after the wheat had been planted, and marched against the Russians. With the Sultan leading them, the men walked unafraid as they met and defeated the Russians, killing 20 or even 50 of them for each Turk who died. The Russians became very much afraid and started to run. They ran far back into Russia, and the Sultan's army followed them. They ran without stopping all the way to the edge of the Caspian Sea, but even running is very slow across the mountains, and by this time it was beginning to get cold. In those days the army did not take food with it as it does today, but ate off the land. The Russians had already eaten most of what was there before the Sultan's army arrived, and when the Turks came after them, there was nothing left. Knowing that he had completely beaten the Russians, the Sultan ordered his men to turn back toward home, and shortly after it began to snow and the wind blew, and it got colder and colder. As the Turkish army made its way over the cold barren wastes of Russia, there was no food at all, none. At night they slept on the cold ground, if they could sleep at all, and by day they suffered from hunger. The men had already eaten everything edible they carried. Finally, they were reduced to eating their shoes, belts, and other things that had any food value. When even this was gone, many starved to death. Of course a few had also been killed by the Russian soldiers. When they arrived back at our village, over half of the men were gone. My father said that he had walked the last few miles barefooted, because he had eaten his shoes along the way.

"Can one really eat his shoes, Grandfather?" one of the smaller boys asked.

"If you get hungry enough," the old man laughed.

"Tell us about the time Hoca borrowed the pans, Grandfather," one of the other young men asked.

"All right."

One day Nesreddin Hoca wanted to make some *pilaf,* so he went to his neighbor and borrowed a pan. After making the *pilaf,* and waiting several days, he brought two pans back to the man.

Surprised to see an extra pan, the neighbor said, "Hoca Efendi, where did the second pan come from?"

"Efendı," replied the Hoca. "You are a lucky man, your pan had a baby."

The neighbor wondered about the Hoca, but since the old man was widely known for his foolishness, the man took the two pans and forgot the incident.

Some time later, Nesreddin Hoca came again to his neighbor's house, and this time he borrowed both pans at the same time. Many days passed, and when Hoca did not return the pans, the neighbor came to inquire about them.

"Hoca Efendi, where are my pans you borrowed some days ago?"

"Oh, my friend, I have sad news for you."

"Oh? What is that?" the neighbor asked, a little puzzled.

"I am so sorry, but your pans have died," responded the Hoca.

"Died?" asked the neighbor.

"Yes, died," repeated the Hoca.

"But how can a pan die? Pans aren't alive," the neighbor protested strongly.

"They just died. You made no complaint when I told you that your pan had a baby. A pan that can have a baby can surely die," the Hoca said quite simply and turned and walked away leaving his neighbor puzzling over what had just happened.

"And now, before anyone asks for another special story, I want to tell one that I like to tell. This is a story about the Dull Knife."

A very, very long time ago there lived in the country an old mother with three daughters and a son.

One day the old mother said to her youngest daughter, "Daughter, I am making bread. Water is needed. Run to the fountain and fill these two water jars."

The young girl took the pots and went to the fountain. Near the fountain she found a small, old knife. Taking the knife in her hand, she turned it over and looked at it carefully. Then she thought to herself, if I take this home with me, and if my older brother gets married and a son is born, the knife will become his. Later, if the son dies, no one will own this knife, and every time I see it, I will have to cry and cry. This pain will be very bitter. At this thought the girl took the two water jars and smashed them together and broke them. Then she sat down and began to cry bitterly.

The mother of the girl wondered what had happened to the water she had sent for and gave two more jars to the middle daughter and said, "your sister has been gone for a long time. Go and look for her, and while you are there fill these two jugs with water."

The middle daughter went to the fountain where she found her younger sister crying.

"What happened? Why are you crying?" the older daughter asked of the young one.

The younger girl told her sister about her thoughts concerning her older brother's son, and the older girl said, "Aman! my sister. If our brother's son dies in this way, who will cry for him if his aunts do not." Then she too smashed her two water jars together and sat down to cry.

The old mother wondered also about the two daughters and gave two more jars to the oldest daughter and sent her to the fountain, saying, "Go and look for your sisters, and while you are going, fill these two jugs with water."

The oldest daughter went and found the other two girls at the fountain crying. She wondered why the girls were crying and asked them. They told the same story to the oldest girl who also smashed her two jugs together and broke them. Then she sat down and began to cry with the other two.

Finally, the old mother, becoming very puzzled, took two more jugs and went to the fountain herself and found the girls crying there together.

"Why are you all crying?" she asked.

The older girl began to explain, and the mother too was grieved by the sorrowful tale and immediately banged her two jugs together, breaking them into pieces, and began to cry also.

Then she said, "Let us go quickly and kill the pregnant cow at the house. Tomorrow the neighbors will come to say, 'Başınıza sag olsun.' Let us go and prepare food for them." They went to the house, killed the cow, and began to prepare food for the neighbors who would come the following day to offer their condolences.

That evening, the old woman's son, after having put the sheep in the barn, saw and wondered about all the confusion in the house.

"I hope that it is good news that causes the excitement," he said questioningly.

The anxious mother and sisters began to pour out their sorrows. They explained the whole thing, and the son became violently angry because the crazy ones had killed his pregnant cow which would have given birth in just a few days.

After a few moments he said, "I have decided to take my head and go away from here. If I can find three people in the world who are crazier than you are, when I come back again, I will not do anything to you. If I do not find three people crazier than you, then when I return, I will kill all of you," and he started on his way.

As he walked quickly by a village, a woman came out and asked, "Son, where are you going in such a hurry?"

The boy answered, "I'm going deep into hell."

This poor country woman believed what he said.

"Son, my son, Ali, is in heaven. Do you know him?"

The young man stopped and looked at the ignorant woman and said, "Yes, I know him. What do you want?"

She answered, "I wanted to ask . . . I have been wondering if my son has money or doesn't have money."

The young man said, "I saw your son while passing, and he doesn't have any money at all."

The woman ran, in great haste, and gave the boy the money they had been saving for a year to buy an ox. The boy took the money and started on his way to a new and different place. He looked back and saw a horse coming full speed. He understood the situation immediately and sat down on the ground and began to walk on his hands as if his legs were broken. The rider stopped and said, "my son, did you see a man walking very fast up this road?"

"Yes, I saw him, uncle, just a little while ago. A man passed this way, running."

"Aman, my son, this man cheated me out of my money." I guess that you are unable to walk, so take this horse and ride after him. I will run along behind you."

The young man got on the horse and said, "Goodbye. I am the man," and started on his way as quickly as he could.

At the side of the road, he met a farmer who was working very hard.

"Greetings, father, I am very hungry and also very thirsty. If you will bring me a pan of steaming *pilaf* (rice) and some very cold *ayran* (similar to buttermilk), I will give you ten gold pieces," he said.

The man ran quickly into his house. He couldn't find his wife in the house, because she was visiting a neighbor. He went to the neighbor's house, found his wife, took a good big stick, and hit his wife on the head several times. The poor little creature, in this condition, made some *pilaf* and *ayran* and gave it to her husband. The husband ran quickly back as he had come, but when he arrived back at the place where the boy had been, he could find nothing. The boy had gone and taken his ox with him as he went.

Oh, well, thought the man, it is of no importance, and he went back to his house, found his wife, and began to beat her on the head.

Our young man, on his way, passed a butcher shop and sold the ox. Filling both sides of his bag with gold, he went on his way again. Then passing another village, he met a wedding party. He saw the bride who was very beautiful.

The boy walked toward the wedding party and in a very loud voice said, "Do you know that it is raining gold on the other side of this mountain?"

Everyone came to the side of the stranger and asked, "Gold?"

The young man opened his bag and said, "I gathered this gold on the other side of the mountain. Over there the rocks are solid gold."

The members of the wedding party chose an old woman from their number, and they said, "We are going to the other side of the mountain to gather gold. While we are gone, you wait with the bride. Later we will all give you a little bit of our gold."

With these words, they sent the old woman to the bride's side and ran directly for the distant mountain.

When the group was a little way away, our young man got down from his horse and said to the old woman, "Why do you wait here, aunt? Look, everyone will gather gold and be rich. No one will give gold to you. Go and gather some too. I will watch the bride."

The old woman too took a bag in her hand and ran. Our young man put the bride behind him on his horse and went full speed back to his own village. When he arrived home, he apologized to his mother and sisters, and there followed a beautiful wedding.

By this time everyone was getting very tired, and one of the older boys came over to Mahmud, took him by the shoulder, and motioned for him to go out. They went into the kitchen together and prepared Turkish coffee. Whenever four or five cups of coffee were ready to go, Mahmud would take them on a tray and offer them first to the oldest man who had not been served, then the next oldest, and so on, until finally all of the men had coffee. The rest of the evening was filled with friendly chatter, and the group broke up very late and went home, only to reassemble at the same time and place the following evening for another similar session, as these gatherings were nearly a nightly affair during the cold months of winter.

5

Subsistence

THE COLD HARD WINTER passed, and most of the people had enough to eat and lived to see the spring. Some died, of course, but the villagers rarely knew why. Malnutrition, caused by lack of variety in their diets during the long cold months, poor sanitation, and living in practically unheated houses combined to cause the death of some. So far as the people could see there were no solutions to these problems, for it had always been so, and when anyone asked why, they were always given the answer that it was the will of Allah.

One morning, after the snows had gone, but the bitter cold winds were still blowing across the hills, his father was fastening the heavy wooden yoke onto the oxen when Mahmud came into the room that was reserved for the animals.

"Let's go together and plow this morning, my son," the older man said.

"What can I do, my father?" the boy responded with enthusiasm.

"You can best watch today, my son, but soon you must help, for you will some day have to plow the fields alone."

The tongue of the wooden plow was fastened securely to the yoke, which was now tightened about the necks of the oxen, and father and son left the village with the two animals dragging the plow on its side. Walking slowly, they proceeded toward a spot high in the neighboring hills, about three miles from the house, where they would prepare the land for planting wheat.

As they walked along, Mahmud examined the plow very carefully, because he knew that one day he would probably have to make one like it. At school they had seen pictures of large plows with steel blades, some of which were even pulled by large machines called tractors, but his father's plow was different. Some wealthy villagers had small steel plows, and new ones came to the country every year. The wooden plow was made from a single log that had once been a fork in a tree. The tree had been cut down, the bark stripped from it, and the two heavy branches that formed the Y-like juncture, became the tongue and single handle, while the trunk of the tree became the plow-

26

share. The latter end had been cut to shape, hardened in fire while still green, and then allowed to dry completely. This was the only piece of equipment that they would need that day, as it would take about a month, working from sunup till sundown, to plow the four acres that his father had decided he would cultivate this year. Whenever he finished turning the soil, he would replace the plow with a heavy log and ride this, behind the same pair of oxen, over the field several times to break up the heavy clods and shake stones loose from the dirt. However, the first and most difficult job was to break the hard-packed, rocky ground so that the seeds could take root and grow.

It took the two of them well over an hour to reach the spot to be planted, and the sun was well up in the sky when they arrived. They did not begin to plow immediately, because the ground had to be cleared of the larger rocks first. This made it much easier for the oxen to pull the dull wooden plowshare through the very hard earth. Picking up the stones, which ranged in size from that of an acorn to a small melon and which lay scattered thickly over the surface of the ground, they made neat piles of rock outside the area to be plowed. These stacks began to look like small buildings, and Mahmud liked to pretend that these structures were the houses of a village of little people, and he made up all kinds of stories about what happened to these people.

By shortly after the noon hour they had cleared nearly half an acre, which was twice as much as a man could plow up in one day, so Mahmud sat down to rest, and his father took up the plow and began the long hard job of following the oxen back and forth across what would soon be his wheat field.

Days passed, each very much like the first, and all of the rocks were cleared from the surface. The ground was broken, and Mahmud followed his father and picked up many more stones that had been turned up during the plowing. Finally, after all this had been done, and his father had decided that they had broken all the land that he and his family could properly tend that year, Mahmud was allowed to ride on the clod-breaking log (harrow). His body added weight to the implement, which made it more efficient, and also gave father and son a chance to work more closely together so that Mahmud could learn how to be a man.

When finally the earth was prepared for planting, Mahmud followed his father as the latter stepped rhythmically over the land and with wide even sweeps of his hand and arm broadcast the wheat seeds evenly over the broken earth. Then the harrow was once more dragged over the field in order to cover the seed with a thin layer of soil, and the crop was left in the hands of Allah until the earth was green when the tiny blades protruded above the ground. At this point Mahmud's father did no more except go every day or so to look at the young plants and see how they were progressing. This was a very good year, as Allah had caused the cool winter winds to linger long into spring and sent light showers to brighten up the plants each time Mahmud's father began to worry about them. Finally the crop was grown, and the heads were full of bright, heavy grain that began to turn a rich golden color, indicating that soon the stalks would be ready to be cut.

When it was time to begin the harvest, the entire family went into the fields, each member equipped with a small sickle, one of the few iron implements owned by the family. This tool was shaped like a very thin crescent moon, about two feet in length, with a wooden handle on it about five inches long. With this grasped firmly in their right hands, the older members of the household spent the days in a semicrouched position cutting the grain. The stalks were not allowed to fall to the ground, but each harvester grasped a bunch of wheat in his left hand and cut this bunch off just above the ground with his sickle. These handfuls were piled together in stacks at random on the field, and later, after they had a few days to dry, they would be picked up and moved to the threshing grounds near the village. For the present, however, the preoccupation of everyone was in getting the stalks cut and ready to move before the wind, birds, or rain came and knocked the grain from its husks. If this happened, a great deal of the harvest would fall to the ground, where it would either furnish food for the birds or sink back into the barren soil.

Many days passed as the cutting progressed and the early cuttings dried there in the field, but finally the day came when this job was finished and Mahmud began helping his father attach a hayrack to the oxcart, the one all-purpose vehicle owned by every village family. This conveyance was constructed in much the same manner as the log-hauling wagon described earlier, only it had a large flat wooden platform on top. The solid wooden wheels, the square axle, and the tongue were all the same. The hayrack consisted of two long poles that were lashed to the platform in the shape of a large V, the small end of which was affixed to the center of the platform on the back of the cart, and the large end was extended toward the front and upward at an angle of something like 30° and supported by two shorter wooden poles that were attached to the front. This arrangement, simple as it seems, allowed an enormous amount of the cut wheat to be carried to the village at one time.

After the hayrack had been attached, there was once more the long tiring trip to the wheat field, then the job of piling the loose stalks on the wagon with crude wooden haying forks. Not too long ago each villager had made these tools for himself, but now they were mass-produced and sold cheaply in the nearby city. These looked something like a large wooden shovel with three u-shaped slits cut into them.

When the hay had been piled so high on the wagon that it looked like a haystack with two wheels on it, the long return trip was started. This was very difficult because there were no roads; each cart just took the shortest route across the rough hillsides, and the large stones and ditches along the way made an overturn very likely. Mahmud and his father had gone less than half the distance to the village when they drew alongside an overturned wagon of one of their neighbors and stopped for a short time to help them refill it. They could not, however, stay until the job was completed, because they had their own wheat to care for. Therefore, after placing a good deal of the spilled hay back onto the wagon, Mahmud and his father wished their neighbors well and went on about their business, which was getting their own wheat back to the village. It was nearly dark when they reached home and emptied the cart near the threshing floor.

These threshing floors were circular areas about 30 feet in diameter where the earth had been packed as hard as stone by centuries of threshing. The newly cut wheat was placed in a large ring around the outside of this area, and early the next morning Mahmud was helping to spread an even layer of the cut wheat over the floor to be threshed.

When just the right amount had been strewn about, the threshing sled was brought out of the house and hitched up to the oxen. The latter implement was very much like a sled. It was made from a single sheet of wood, turned up at the front end, with sharp pieces of obsidian or other similar volcanic stone embedded in the bottom. Mahmud, his mother, and the baby rode this implement round and round the threshing floor until the straw turned a different color, and was cut up into much smaller pieces. Then it was raked into a pile in the center of the circle, and a new layer of straw was strewn over the floor.

This process was repeated again and again until there was a large pile of threshed wheat in the center. Whenever there was a good wind, loads of this material was carried to one side and winnowed, a process whereby a large amount of the threshed wheat was thrown up into the air and the chaff blown some distance away by the wind while the grains of wheat settled to the ground. The wheat was then swept up and put into large bags where it would be kept safely until it was needed. The excess, over what the family would require for seed the following year and food during the winter months, was taken to the government warehouse and sold to the wheat monopoly for cash. The chaff was used alone for fuel or mixed with manure to make it burn better, while the straw was fed to the animals, mixed with mud to make stronger bricks, or perhaps burned if there was any excess, which was very unusual.

These weeks of early summer were hard on everyone, and even Mahmud worked so steadily, for there was always some simple job that he could do, that he hardly had time to think about anything except the work of harvesting. When all the grain had been cut, threshed, and separated from the chaff, it was laid out, either on the ground or the roof, on large sheets of cotton cloth to dry. The hot Anatolian sun made quick work of this, and soon the kernels were hard, and could be safely stored away in the house until they were needed for flour.

One day soon after the harvest was completed and there was no other pressing work, Mahmud and his father took two large sacks of wheat, loaded them on the back of their strongest donkey, and started toward the flour mill that was built on a small stream about five miles from the village. It took a long time for them to reach this distant place, and Mahmud loved to listen to his father talk along the way, though he understood little of what was being said most of the time. It was very pleasant to walk slowly along behind the donkey across the hills. The sun was very hot even in the early morning, but there was a cool breeze, and one must always suffer the heat of the sun in summer. Here and there they passed a fountain, where they would stop, water the donkey, get a drink for themselves, and throw cold water into their faces in order to be refreshed for the rest of the trek.

After they had walked a long way, they saw the mill in the distance. It looked to Mahmud like some sort of monster with its large funnel-shaped water chute running down the side of the mountain from a small stream.

Inside the rough, unpainted wooden structure, the old miller sat on a log while the scraping of the upper millstone, which turned against the lower one, ground the wheat kernels into a fine white powder, mixed of course with a few grains of sand from the mill itself. Every so often the old miller would get up, take a small tin container of wheat (actually an American beer can with a handle soldered onto it) from a bag nearby and pour it into a hole in the center of the revolving stone disk. Then he would dust some of the newly ground flour from around the edges of the two stones into the same container and dump this into a white bag near at hand.

When Mahmud and his father came up, the old man greeted them and wished them well. Then the two men talked for a while as the bag of wheat that was being ground was emptied. Then Mahmud's father opened his bags and replaced the empty one on the floor with one of his own. They had been lucky enough to be the first new customers for that day, but long before their bag was finished, many other men and donkeys came up, singly and in groups, from distant villages, a few with young boys Mahmud's age. The boys ran away to play on top of a nearby hill from which they could see a great distance in every direction, and when another boy appeared with his father, they would run to meet him long before he reached the mill.

The men sat in the shade of the trees and talked about their villages, the weather, or about politics. The new government had promised to do great things for the villagers, and many thought that they would, but some were not so sure, and so they talked. It might have seemed logical for Mahmud's father to leave early, since his grain was ground long before the time for midday prayers. However, this was of no consequence to either his father or to any of the other men, and Mahmud ran happily about with his newly found friends. He knew that he would not leave until past the middle of the afternoon, for his father would talk and talk and talk with the men he had not seen for many months and some that he had never seen before. This was more than just a trip to have the flour ground; it was a social occasion that gave his father a chance to hear about the goings-on in distant villages.

Finally, however, midafternoon did come, and they started the long journey back home. Instead of the two brown bags of freshly dried wheat kernels, this time the donkey carried a single bag of newly ground flour. A portion of the flour had gone to the miller for his services, and then the ground wheat did not take up as much space as had the dry kernels.

6

Digging a Well

AROUND THE VILLAGE there are irrigation canals wherever there is water. These ditches require almost constant attention from the men, and one day Mahmud went to watch his father deepen a ditch near their little garden. Here they were growing eggplant, onions, garlic, melons, beans, squash, and tomatoes, and all needed to be watered almost daily.

As soon as they reached the small plot, Mahmud's father began to dig an already existing irrigation canal a little deeper. This activity interested Mahmud, as it did all the boys, and he watched for a long time as the now dry bed grew deeper and deeper. His father dug away with a small hand axe, picking up the rocks and tossing them into a neat pile beside the canal as he went along.

Suddenly, the heretofore dry ground seemed to spring a leak, or so Mahmud thought, as a thin stream of water began to spurt upward and form a tiny pool around the spot where Mahmud's father had just cut into the earth with his axe. He redoubled his efforts and in a very short time there was a fairly large stream of cold, clear water bubbling up out of the hole, and Mahmud and his father ran off to tell the villagers that they had found a new spring.

This may not seem important to those who live in a benign climate where there is plenty of rainfall, but to semidesert dwellers this spells life and death for many. It has been said that one of the principal limiting factors to the size of a community in the Middle East is the water supply, so this good news was well received by the other members of the town. This meant that more land could be irrigated, more gardens grown, and more marketable produce raised to sell in the city and to eat whenever they needed it.

Permitting the water to simply bubble up and flow out into his irrigation ditches, Mahmud's father went first to the Muhtar, as he should be the first to know, since the entire village was the responsibility of this old man. Then Mahmud's father told the other men in the town that he would build a new stone fountain there.

Returning to the garden only long enough to determine that the water was indeed running about the plants and not being wasted, his father went to the nearby city that very afternoon, bought cement, and the next morning began to collect building stones from the surrounding mountains. In a few days all was ready, and with the help of his closest friends Mahmud's father cemented the stones together to form a rectangular structure about four feet above the ground, ten feet in length, and two feet thick. Four new iron pipes were fastened in between the stones in a straight line. Finally, the top was cemented over to force the freely flowing water to come out of the pipes, and the village had a new fountain, from which spouted four strong streams of water.

Since this spring had come right out in the middle of one of the old ditches, it was not going to be much of a job to connect it into the already existing irrigation system. Still a few new canals would have to be dug, and this was not the responsibility of Mahmud's father. It had been his civic duty to build the fountain, though there would have been no censure if he had not, but at most his duty ended there. Maintaining the large arteries of the canal system was the responsibility of the entire village, and the Muhtar would assign several of the older boys and young men to connect this new supply into the old system. Once or twice each year the Muhtar would have to request that the young men repair the canals, and it was always done, despite the resistance of a few.

The smaller ditches, which ran to the individual plots, were kept up by the owners of the gardens. Though Mahmud's father had found the spring and built the fountain, he had no more claim on the water than did any of his neighbors. After all, had it not been sent by Allah for the use of all His children.

The new supply of water had come at just the proper time, for the garden vegetables had not had enough water. Before the villagers connected the fountain into the larger irrigation systems, Mahmud's father had profited greatly by letting the water run continuously into his own garden.

Before long Mahmud was helping his mother and sisters as they gathered large basketfuls of tomatoes, eggplant, and other vegetables. All this was very good for Mahmud's father, for he took the baskets, woven from strips of poplar bark, to the city where he sold the vegetables at the market place.

Mahmud's father was very grateful to Allah for sending the water, because before the summer was over he had paid back all of the money that he had had to borrow from the other villagers for Fatma's wedding. This was very unusual. Many men had to labor for years before they were lucky enough to have paid off all the marriage debts, even for one child. This was good, not only because Mahmud's father was out of debt, but the sale of the vegetables left a little money for the wedding of Mahmud's older brother Ali. It was decided also to sell a little more of the wheat from the spring harvest. They would then turn all the money into gold to save for the wedding that they planned to arrange for the coming summer.

When all the excess vegetables and wheat had been sold, Mahmud's father went to the jewelry shop in the city and changed the paper bank notes into thin bands of pure gold, which were sold by weight. These he brought back to the village, and his wife wore them on her arms at all times, lest they should be lost.

There was a bank in the city, but Mahmud's father knew little of these institutions, and he preferred the old method of keeping his money where he knew that it would be safe, on his wife's person. If during the coming year they were to need money for food, he could take one or two of the bracelets into the city and exchange them at the going price of gold for cash, so these were as good as food. They could not spoil or be carried away by the rats or insects, which were a constant menace to the stored foods of the villagers.

7

The Preparation of Foods

IN GENERAL, the village was not a money-making place. The peasants consumed most of what they produced. Occasional surpluses of wheat or vegetables were sold in the city, but this amounted to very little, both in value and percentage of total production. Therefore, despite the fact that many baskets of vegetables had been strapped onto the back of their faithful donkey and hauled off to town, most of the vegetables were cooked by Mahmud's mother and sisters and eaten by the family and their friends.

Each morning Mahmud's mother would collect the makings for whatever she planned to cook that day and begin to prepare the vegetables for cooking. Mahmud usually paid little attention to "women's work." However, one morning he found himself with nothing in particular to do and he became aware of the noises coming from the kitchen.

Fatma, the oldest daughter, was married and had gone to live with her in-laws. It was the custom to marry the oldest children first and the younger ones in order of age, though there was no strict rule about it. This left Mahmud's two other sisters and his mother to do all the housework. As he came in, the younger of the two girls was pouring water into a circular copper pan about a yard across and eight inches deep. The older girl was alternately pumping up the *pumpa gaz ocak* (a small kerosene stove that works on much the same principle as does the gasoline camp stove) and trying to light it. His mother was collecting a selection of tomatoes, peppers, eggplants, and onions in another large copper pan.

The recipe that Mahmud's mother was following would read something like the one given below were it committed to writing, though she had never written it out, nor indeed could she have read it even if it had been.

Eggplant, Tomato, and Pepper Stuffing

5 cups of rice
5 teaspoons of salt

5 pints of water
¼ pound of butter
2¼ pounds of ground lamb
5 medium onions
5 cups of flour

Needless to say, the above mixture was more than enough for one meal for the family. This would be reheated each day until it had all been eaten up, probably three to four days later. There was no refrigeration in the village, but at this altitude the temperature was very cool at night, even in summer, and cooked food, which was kept in closed containers, rarely spoiled.

When the older girl had fired up the stove, she took the rice, a fairly large pan of it even when still dry, washed it thoroughly, poured it into a pan with about double its volume of water, covered it with a thin copper lid, and waited for it to boil.

In the meantime her younger sister had taken the 40 or so vegetables from her mother and washed them thoroughly. When they were clean, she cut out the stems so that they could later be replaced as if they were small caps and emptied the insides of the vegetables so that these could be stuffed.

Mahmud's mother had taken a large piece of lamb from a wooden box, which protected it from the dirt and insects, and began to chop it very finely with a heavy steel knife, which she had bought in the city many years ago. Then she mixed the meat with flour, salt, and pepper, and turned to see if the rice were boiling yet. Finding that it was not, she turned her hand to helping her girls, who were now both preparing the vegetables. In a few minutes a puff of vapor from the pan of rice told her that this was boiling, so she removed it from the fire, took the lid off, covered the steaming container with a double thickness of clean cotton cloth, and replaced the lid.

The rice was then set aside and left alone as another large pan was placed on the single flame and two or three tablespoons of olive oil poured into it. Then the meat and flour mixture was put in to brown. When the lamb had attained the desired color, Mahmud's mother covered it with water and put a lid on it. This was allowed to simmer while she minced the five onions.

When it was determined that the rice and meat were both cooked sufficiently, they were mixed with the onions. Then the eggplants, tomatoes, and peppers were stuffed lightly with the mixture. Finally, these were placed in a third pan in concentric circles, covered, and allowed to cook.

None of this food would be eaten immediately. It was allowed to cool and put in the storage box from which it would be taken and reheated for the evening meal. Tomorrow evening it would again be reheated, and in this manner the results of the morning's work would last for several days.

Mahmud watched the women cleaning and preparing many other foods as the stuffed vegetables cooked. Grapes grew well in the rocky soil, and these were eaten fresh, or the juice was made into a thick syrup called *pekmez*. This syrup was made by placing the grapes in a cubical container made of thin slabs of flat stone. Then the young men, having washed their feet very carefully, walked on the grapes until the juice was extracted. Mahmud frequently helped to collect the juice from a small hole at the bottom of one end of this device. Then the juice was boiled for a long time, until it formed the *pekmez*.

The grapes, when gathered after several days without rain and when they had grown large and plump, would keep fresh for as long as four months when hung on racks in a cool room or cave. Melons and other vegetables were also kept for long periods of time in this manner, but no canning was practiced in the homes at all.

An interesting beverage was made from rose petals by placing them in a jar of water and allowing this mixture to stand in the sun for several weeks. The liquid derived from this process made a very refreshing drink when suitably diluted and sweetened. Rose petals were also frequently made into marmalade.

Sugar, salt, and spices were bought in the city, and yoghurt, *ayran* (a beverage), and butter were all made in the village by the women. Each day the sheep and goats were milked. The milk was boiled immediately, because the animals were not vaccinated, and while the villagers did not understand this, they knew that people frequently got very sick and sometimes even died from drinking unboiled milk.

Yoghurt was made by placing some of the still warm freshly boiled milk into a pan, adding two or three tablespoons of old yoghurt, and allowing this to stand for about twenty-four hours. This could be eaten just as it was, or mixed with water to make *ayran* (pronounced *I ron*) which tastes vaguely like buttermilk.

The remainder of the boiled milk was then put into the skin of a calf, which had been thoroughly cleaned of all the hair and fat on it. This gruesome fixture hung from a wooden rack in a cool place somewhere in the storeroom, and the natural pores of the skin sweated continuously, so that the milk was kept cool. In a dry climate this is an exceptionally good refrigeration system. As the days passed, this container was gradually filled with milk, in various degrees of souring, and when it was full, the women would empty its contents into pans and shake them gently in an up and down circular motion. This caused the coagulated portions of the milk to separate from the watery whey. The whey was drunk as a beverage in winter or poured on *bulgur* (rough ground wheat that has been boiled), the way Americans put milk on oatmeal. The curds were made into a white cheese that formed a major portion of the villagers breakfast menu. During the shaking process the cream in the mixture collected into lumps of butter, and this was formed into balls and stored away for use in cooking.

Mahmud's mother had been taking various foods from small wooden boxes in the storage room, bringing them to the kitchen, and mixing them with other ingredients as she waited for the stuffed peppers, eggplant, and tomatoes to cook, and vague images of the above operations had flashed erratically through the boy's mind as he watched. However, he grew weary of watching after a time and drifted out the door and slowly along the dry dusty street that ran in front of his father's house. Walking unhurriedly he eventually found his way to the top of a nearby hill from which he could view nearly all of the surrounding countryside. He liked to come here because it somehow made him feel as if he were the king of all the world.

Far toward the north Mahmud could see a group of small stones pointing skyward that looked for all the world as if they were fingers. He remembered the story, told over and over by the men on winter nights, that there had been, long ago, a beautiful bride grazing her sheep on the side of the mountain, for the men had all gone to war and her husband had left her there alone to care for the land and animals. While returning home one evening with her baby in her arms, she saw in the distance the enemy army coming toward her. Becoming very frightened, the young bride held her baby close to her and began to pray to God to change her into a rock or something so that she would not be taken by the enemy soldiers. God looked down from Heaven, took pity on the poor girl, and turned her and her sheep into the field of stones that can still be seen high on the mountain side from the highway as you drive between Ankara and Kaman. Mahmud wondered if God would ever save him if he were in such danger, but boys are not prone to think long on things such as these and so he looked at other things.

Generally northward he could see the city which was not too far away. Occasionally a car would pass slowly down the gravelled highway and disappear into the tightly packed cluster of buildings with their red-tiled roofs. Since he had started school Mahmud had been to the city many times, but to him it was still a different world, not his world at all. The city was a place full of strange people and even stranger things where no one seemed to raise sheep or vegetables, yet they always had more to eat, good clothing, and many other things that the villagers did not have. He did not understand this, but then he did not care very much; it was just a passing thought.

Turning eastward, there was little that he could see there, for the mountains gradually grew in height, and all that appeared above each ridge was another still higher ridge, until finally there was only the sky.

To the south extended the fields of the villagers, all of whom were Mahmud's relatives, and so in a way it all belonged to his family. All of the good land to the edge of the barren hills, which appeared to be a great distance away to a small boy, was cultivated by his cousins and uncles. There was only a single house in this lonely stretch of land. The old Muhtar had a country home there, near his fields. He was the only man in the village now to have two wives, because this was no longer legal in Turkey, but when he had been young, many people had had more than one wife. This man had married twice before the new law had been passed, and so he was allowed to keep both of his wives. Now he had a village home and a country home, one for each of his families.

Near this single dwelling was a very good fountain, and Mahmud could see the network of irrigation canals watering the gardens of this man who was a brother to Mahmud's great grandfather. Surrounding this small plot of green, dotted with a few trees, was a vast desolate area burned brown by the late summer sun after the wheat crop had been cut off.

To the west Mahmud could see a great distance, and the land looked much as it did to the south, except that it gradually swept away to a much lower elevation and the ragged mountains could be seen only very faintly as a grayish outline on the horizon. Much of this land also belonged to his village, but somewhere out there in the distance was an imaginary line, not clearly drawn, separating his village's land from that of the next village. This so-called line was so far away that it was of little concern to Mahmud or, for that matter, to most of the other villagers, as they had plenty of land to till much nearer home. The distance between the village and the fields was an important factor to the people who had to go out to their fields every day on the backs of slow donkeys or, worse even, to walk. The farther one went the less work could be done during the course of the day, for much of the time was taken up with traveling back and forth.

Finally, Mahmud's mind was drawn back to the village, and looking down on his own home, he saw a group of women gathering near the front door. Wondering what they had come for, he focussed his attention very closely on the implements that they carried in their hands. The small tables and rolling pins told him that they had gathered to bake bread. Since this occasion presented itself only once in about three months, and he was not otherwise occupied, he decided to go down and watch. It was woman's work, but it was better than doing nothing at all.

Before Mahmud reached home, his mother came out the front door carrying one of the rolling pins, which was not more than an inch in diameter, and a small table about two and a half feet in length, two feet wide, and perhaps eight inches tall, built on legs that were very much like sled runners. His older sister followed her. The girl was carrying a copper pan about three and a half feet in diameter and about ten inches deep. The interior of this utensil was coated with a thin layer of tin. The younger sister carried a cluster of small bags containing flour, salt, and eggs.

Younger girls accompanied their mothers to do a lot of the legwork and to learn the trade of being a good village housewife at the same time. Mahmud followed the women at some distance, as he did not want any of the older boys teasing him about being with the girls. After a short walk the women went into a small building which, to Mahmud's knowledge, did not belong to anyone. The girls deposited their small bundles inside the door and ran off to fetch water, as the women scattered themselves around the room so that they would not be in each other's way. He watched his mother pour a large quantity of flour into the container that she had had his older sister bring, then break a number of eggs into it, and finally season it with a small amount of salt.

By this time one of the other women had a fire going in a small circular pit in one corner of the room. This oven was so well designed that even though the lid was off there was no smoke in the room. Mahmud watched with wonder as the light grayish white smoke poured out the chimney above the building.

Mahmud's mother chatted idly with one of the women until the girls appeared with their earthenware jars of water. Then she mixed the batter, threw it out onto her mixing board, and passed the pan on to one of the other women who began to mix her dough.

In the meantime the lady tending the fire had placed a large iron dome on top of the oven. Therefore only a very small opening was left at the front of the oven to throw in wood, straw, and/or manure chips to keep the fire going.

Mahmud's mother rolled out a circle of dough about two feet in diameter and less than an eighth-of-an-inch thick. This she lifted gently with two of the rolling pins and placed it on top of the iron dome. As it browned quickly on one side, she rolled out another one. At the same time the other women were mixing and rolling, but without hurry, for this was after all as much a social occasion as it was work. Gossip and chatter took equally as much time as rolling the bread out.

When one side of the bread was baked, Mahmud's mother turned it over, and in just a few minutes it was done on the other side. Then that loaf was taken off and another was put in its place. There was no order, apparently no rhyme or reason in the sequence followed by the women, but there was no bickering, as no one was in any hurry to be done or to go home.

Thus the day passed with the young girls bringing water, running back to the houses for more eggs, flour, or salt, and idly watching. The raw ingredients were gradually turned into piles of thin circular loaves of unleavened bread, and by late afternoon each woman had two or three piles of bread which were almost three feet high, enough for her family for about three months. After which time they would gather again for another day of pleasant work and gossip.

Mahmud had watched only a small portion of the procedure, as a group of boys his age had come by and he had wandered off with them. They had gone out of the village to the grove of poplar trees. There a game of tag had consumed the remaining hours of daylight, and before they knew it the sun was almost touching the horizon. Since they were all hungry, the group disbanded and went toward their respective homes.

As Mahmud walked homeward, he remembered the stuffed peppers that he had seen being prepared in the morning, and the thought of them quickened his steps. When he arrived at the front door of his home, it was nearly dark, and his mother had already set up the small portable table in the hallway near the kitchen entrance. He could smell the food as it was being heated in the other room, so he quickly rinsed the dust off his hands and waited.

A large wooden spoon had been placed on the table for Mahmud, another for his father, and one for each of his brothers. Beside the spoon one of his sisters had put a neatly folded piece of bread, and soon his mother brought a large tray, arranged with stuffed peppers, tomatoes, and eggplants, and set it in the center of the table.

When all the men had arrived, they sat on the floor to eat together. Each ate from the tray in the center with his large spoon, holding the bread beneath it so that no food was spilled. When each had his fill of one thing, he turned his spoon upside down and leaned it against the center dish. When all of the spoons were so arranged, his mother would bring another dish, and so the meal went until the men had eaten their fill. Then the older men retired to the men's room for coffee, which Mahmud served to them. Then while they talked, he wandered outside again to look for some adventure in the darkness while the women set about eating and cleaning up after the evening meal, which was the largest of the day.

8

Leaving for the Army

NOT MANY DAYS after the harvest was in and most of the work for the summer had been completed, Mahmud watched with interest as a jeep bounded up the rough hillside toward the village. Visits by outsiders were infrequent, and Mahmud, along with nearly all of the boys, ran out to meet the vehicle. As it came to a rather sudden stop, he saw that it contained a soldier with two officers, but they were from the Army, not the *Jandarma* (a military organization distinct from the Army and under the control of the Ministry of the Interior), as he had at first thought. The two officers leaped quickly off either side of the jeep as the driver turned the ignition off and secured the hand brake. Mahmud thought that these were indeed fine looking men in their neatly pressed and tailored uniforms. On the shoulders of the one who appeared to be in charge three stars glittered (a captain), but the rank of the second man was marked only by a single star (a second lieutenant). All of the boys saluted sharply as the newcomers approached the group. The soldiers returned the salute and directed a question to Mahmud.

"Where's the Muhtar?"

Mahmud turned back toward the cluster of buildings behind him, spied the Muhtar walking slowly in their direction, and pointed him out. The officer in charge looked at the approaching figure, glanced down at Mahmud and his friends, smiled, ruffled the hair of the boy nearest him, and started off to meet the Muhtar. The officers had come to discuss with him the induction of the young men from the village who were ready to fulfill their military service obligation, something Mahmud would have to do in ten or twelve years. Every Turkish male citizen is required to serve his country, and the normal age for entering this service is about 18, but the determination as to who is to go each year is pretty much the responsibility of the Muhtar, at least in the villages. Mahmud's older brother had reached draft age but was not married as yet, and his parents hoped that he would not be called until the following year.

The two men met the Muhtar near the edge of the village, shook hands,

41

and disappeared with him around the corner of a nearby building. The children clustered about the jeep until they had looked it over several times. Having satisfied their curiosity, the boys moved off in a group to where they knew the officers had gone. As they had expected, the men were sitting in front of the Muhtar's house on three very rickety old unpainted wooden chairs, drinking tea. This beverage was sipped slowly from containers made of a very thin glass, flared at the top and bottom, and decorated with three thin stripes around the narrowed middle. Most Turks prefer these to cups, as one can see both the color and the purity, or impurity, of the liquid within by holding it up to the light.

An hour or so had passed since the arrival of the officers, and it was now nearly noon. The children watched at a distance as the men continued to talk for a short while; then they rose. The Muhtar shook hands with his two guests and walked away, as they resumed their seats to await his return. He was on his way to visit the fathers of the men who would be eligible to be called up for service that fall. Mahmud followed him, remaining quietly outside each house while the Muhtar talked within, until they reached his own home. There he followed the old man inside and listened to the conversation with his father concerning his older brother.

There was a brief, courteous interchange of polite but meaningless talk, then the Muhtar told Mahmud's father that his oldest son would have to come that afternoon to the men's room of the Muhtar's home for a physical examination by the Army doctors. The father agreed, but mentioned the problem of his son's not being married and asked that the Muhtar come back in a few days to discuss the possibility of having his son held over until the following year so that he could be properly married before leaving the village. It was considered to be very unwise for young men to go into the service without being married first, because they might go running with loose women in the cities near the Army camps, or perhaps, even worse, they might marry someone from outside the village. The Muhtar agreed that he would at least come back and discuss the matter, and then went on about the job of informing the other family heads.

Shortly after the noon prayers all of the 18-year-olds (usually less than 10 in a small village) began to gather around the Muhtar's house. Most of them did not know exactly when they were born, nor did their parents, because this was of no real importance to them. It was enough to know approximately when to start school, when to be circumcised, when to be married, and when to go into the Army, but a year or two one way or the other was of no importance whatsoever.

The government had required doctors to file birth certificates for many years, but most of the mothers had not been attended by a physician (even in 1960), and therefore the necessary papers had not been filled out and deposited at the government offices in the city. The memories of the parents were not exact, but they were thought to be good enough for village purposes.

After the men had gathered all of them were given a thorough physical examination. At the completion the youths were allowed to go home and the two officers shook hands again with the Muhtar, collected their papers, and left the village shortly before dark. Mahmud watched them leave and wondered if his brother would have to go into the Army that year or the next.

A few days later the Muhtar came to see Mahmud's father, and the boy sat on the floor in a corner of the room as the two men had a long discussion about his older brother's situation. Both men agreed that the boy was old enough and that this was really the proper year for him to enter the service, but his father made a strong plea for his being deferred until the next year. This the Muhtar accepted, and it was decided that if the marriage were arranged as soon as possible, so that by the time the officers came the following year the boy would be ready to go, he would not be called that summer. After reaching this decision, there was a lengthy conversation about this and that before the Muhtar finally rose and left to go home.

It was of little consequence either to the Army or to the village just when a man did his service, as he could not escape it for long, and the community did not have a specific quota to fill. Therefore these things were easily arranged so long as everyone dealt with the Muhtar in good faith, which they almost always did. Even if the promised wedding did not come about, the man's service would probably be postponed again the following year and no one would care. However, the wedding was arranged that fall, in the same manner as it had been for Ayşe, only that the girl's parents initiated the action rather than Mahmud's, and the following spring his brother was married. The young bride and groom had lived together hardly two months when the officers came that summer to tell him that it was nearly time for him to go away. His service would last for two years, during which time he might not get home at all.

The new bride in Mahmud's home was of some interest to him, for she was always on the run. When there was work in the kitchen to be done, he heard his mother's voice snapping out the word *gelin* (bride) almost constantly, always followed by a command to do this or that about the house. When the men (even Mahmud) ate, or simply wanted something, they would sing out, "Gelin," bring this or that. Thus she ran from morning till night, trying to satisfy her new family and prove that she was a good housewife. There was no hope that things would improve for her in the near future either. This situation would remain unchanged until Mahmud married and brought a new *gelin* into the house, or if Mahmud's brother released his wife from her semi-servant status three or four years later, after she had born a son. Then she would be on the same footing with Mahmud's sisters so far as the work about the house was concerned.

The physical examinations were completed as they had been the previous year, and some weeks later another officer came, this one alone, to talk with those men who had been selected to go. Mahmud accompanied his older brother and stood about watching as the Army man called the recruits over to his desk one at a time. His brother was the third one in line, and Mahmud heard the officer ask his name. When he had given it, a large envelope containing a thick stack of papers was fished out from a small portable file. When the paper with Mahmud's brother's name on it had been found, the officer pulled it out and asked the youth to sit down. Then the older man asked him if he could read and write, and when the boy stated that he could, he was asked to write his name. This he did, and he was then labeled "literate." This meant that he would go directly into the basic military training program and not into one of the special literacy schools that the Army was running for illiterate recruits. Then his brother answered all sorts of questions and Mahmud's mind wandered for a long period of time during the questioning. Finally, the officer rose and shook hands with the young man, and the two brothers left for home.

In the following weeks Mahmud's mother and the *gelin* made all sorts of things for his brother to take with him to the Army. The boy's father gave him a lot of advice, most of which was 22 years out-dated, about how to behave. Then finally the day came for the family to say goodbye. After the women had wept, said "Maşallah" over and over many times, the three men left the house and Mahmud and his father went down with his brother to the road near the edge of the city to wait for the bus to Ankara.

The air was still, and it was hot, and the dust lay undisturbed while the men stood patiently beside the small wooden suitcase in which Mahmud's brother carried all sorts of things to eat and wear, most of which he would not be able to use in the Army anyway. But he did not know this at the time.

As they watched down the road for the bus, they talked somewhat uneasily. Mahmud did not want to see his brother go, nor did the old man. The young man waited with a mixture of fear and anticipation, for he had never been farther from the village than the city, which he could see in the distance.

Finally a large cloud of dust billowing above the highway indicated that the bus was coming. Mahmud kissed his brother sadly on each cheek, and wished God would give him a pleasant journey. Then the young man kissed his father on both cheeks. By this time the bus was coming to a halt, and the huge cloud of dust that had been following the vehicle now completely covered the bus, all the passengers, and the three men on the side of the road as well. Looking at the carrier they saw that not only was there no room on the inside, but men sat on top and hung onto the ladder coming down the side of the bus. Mahmud's brother said a few parting words as he paid the driver the fare. Then he threw his suitcase on top of the bus and tried to find a place to hang on to, at least until someone got off.

A few minutes later the bus pulled out, and Mahmud and his father stood by the side of the road and waved until it was out of sight before turning and walking slowly back toward the village. For a while the house would be a sad place because Mahmud's older brother had been like a second father to him, and naturally the old man would miss his first son, who had been at home for over 19 years.

9

The Mosque School

ONE MORNING, not long after his brother had left for the Army, Mahmud trudged wearily toward the village mosque. In the distance he could see the tall thin spire of the minaret in the nearby city, but this graceful structure of new brick and mortar, rising high above a barely visible red-tiled roof, stood in stark contrast to the village's simple wooden platform covered by a small roof of planks and surrounded by a rough, unpainted, hand-carved banister. This stand was built at one edge of the mud-brick building, just above the level of the roof. Though these two structures were different, they served a single purpose. At almost the same hours, five times each day, the Hocas mounted the platforms and called their flocks to pray.

From the outside the village *cami* (mosque) looked much like the buildings around it. It was somewhat taller, square rather than rectangular, and a little larger than the homes, but it was built in the same manner and of identical materials. The momentary thought that this was not a very elegant place to go to learn about Allah flitted through Mahmud's mind. Remembering the pictures in his school books of the Sultan Ahmet Cami (the blue mosque) in Istanbul, made of large stones with its huge domes, six minarets, beautiful blue and green tiles, and stained-glass windows, it was impossible to escape the unfavorable comparison with these undecorated mud-brick walls, the flat mud roof, the small clear-glass windows, and hardly a minaret at all. This contrast did not bother him very much, however, for he already knew that city people had a great many things that the villagers either lacked altogether or had in poorer quality. Questions concerning this situation when addressed to the old people always evoked the answer that it was the will of Allah, and so his mind passed on to things of more import to a young boy.

Mahmud was on his way to school that morning. Not the regular school in the city, for it was still summer vacation and there would be no one there, but to the religious classes given by the Hoca so that the children might have a chance to learn their prayers and some of the verses in the Koran. These were not taught in the Ministry of Education schools. Ataturk, the founder of the Turkish Republic, had felt that one of the most important reforms in Turkey had to be the strict separation of church and state. Therefore religious classes in the public schools had been outlawed, along with the wearing of the fez and the veil, though most of the village women still wore the latter in the presence of strange men.

As Mahmud reached the building, he could hear the others, mostly children about his own age and a few young adults, reciting the sing-song strains of the Koran. Slipping off his shoes and creeping quietly inside the door, he folded his legs beneath him and sat down. Looking up toward the Hoca, who had apparently not been disturbed by his entrance, Mahmud was relieved not to be scolded for coming so late.

The inside of the building was simply a large empty room with blue Arabic writing here and there on the whitewashed walls. In the right-hand corner as one faced away from the entrance stood a small wooden platform that could be reached by going up about ten feet of unpainted stairway. Perched at the top of this was a small square room, about two and a half feet wide and five feet in height covered with a pyramidal roof. The back and sides were covered with thin sheets of wood, and a piece of dark red velvet hung down over the front. The wooden portions were covered with very crude, hand-carved designs of leaves and flowers. The whole thing was unpainted, and the hand-rail had been worn smooth through years of use.

Each wall of the *cami,* with the exception of the one facing Mecca, had two small squarish windows. The side that faced the Moslem holy-land was solid, and in the center was an undecorated niche. The entire floor was covered with thick, hand-woven, brightly-colored carpets on which the Hoca and his pupils were sitting.

Above and just behind the students was a balcony, which was protected from view in the front by an unpainted wooden lattice. This was the place where the women could see the Hoca and worship unveiled without being seen by strange men. There were hardly ever any women in the mosque, however, as they usually said their prayers at home, and they seldom attended the Friday services.

Hanging from the ceiling were some small glass globes, which could be filled with olive oil. Protruding from the open tops of these containers were small wicks which, when ignited, could provide light for services in the evenings. This unusual chandelier was suspended from the center of the roof by a wrought-iron, spider-web-like framework in the shape of an inverted cone. There was also a recently added electric bulb hanging from the center of this fixture. No one had bothered to take out the old lamps, but they had not been used at all in the past two years.

Having observed the physical appearance of the building, Mahmud now turned to look at the students, both boys and girls, around him. The pupils were sitting at random in front of the Hoca, and each attempted as best he could to repeat what the teacher had just said. The exact reproduction of each phrase was thought to be exceedingly important, but the din coming from the assemblage sounded like total chaos. An outside observer might well have wondered how anyone could tell exactly what the Hoca had said, let alone imitate him.

One among many problems was the fact that learning the prayers was very much like learning jibberish. The students were repeating Arabic, not Turkish, and none of them knew what they were saying. The whinelike chant from the leader sounded a little like singing to Mahmud, rather than talking, but he knew that he was not supposed to understand. These were prayers and they had to be repeated perfectly in Arabic if one wanted to be sure that Allah understood them. Therefore each of the children tried to learn them as perfectly as he could.

The Hoca was dressed very much like everyone else in the village, except that his regular clothing was covered by a special robe that was heavily decorated with silver and gold embroidery. Beneath this he wore a pair of very dark trousers that were similar to riding pants. In the mosque his feet were covered only with a pair of heavy, white, hand-woven woolen stockings, but when outside he wore shoes that had been bought in the nearby city. Above the waist he wore a colored shirt of European style, but cut to a slightly different pattern, with the collar buttoned and no tie. Over this he wore a heavy hand-woven woolen vest that had no sleeves and was buttoned down the front. About his waist was a bright band of cloth, wound several times around his middle, which gave him a rather lumpy appearance. Finally, a turban of colored cloth was wound tightly about his head.

The learning of verses and prayers from the Koran went on for some time before the Hoca stopped and began explaining to the children some of the things about their religion in Turkish, a language in which Mahmud could at least partially understand the concepts. Some of the holidays described, such as the one celebrated on the day Mohammed had been conceived, were vague in Mahmud's mind, but he did understand the five pillars on which the Moselm religion rested. He understood quite well that first he must give to the poor whenever he saw a need. It did not have to be much, but he should give whatever he could, because this was one of the commandments of the Prophet. Second, he was to pray five times a day, at sunrise, midmorning, noon, midafternoon, and at sunset. Third, he was supposed to fast during the holy month of *Ramazan* (*Ramadan* in Arabic) from shortly before sunrise to sometime after sunset. This fasting was to be complete, no food or water, no smoking or drinking, and no women, something that at Mahmud's age was also, to say the least, somewhat vague. Fourth, he was supposed to kill a sheep and feed the poor on the *Kurban Bayram* (sacrifice holiday). Fifth, he was to make the holy pilgrimage to Mecca where he would change his clothes for holy garments, pray, fast, and symbolically throw all of his sins away by tossing rocks at the huge black stone in Mecca. Then, when he went to the life after death, he would be accountable only for those sins that he had committed after his *Hacı* (pilgrimage), and thereafter he would be given the title and called Hacı Mahmud. However, hardly anyone in the village had ever been able to make the pilgrimage, because it was very expensive, and the villagers did not make the amount of money required for this kind of trip.

After a rather long session, part of which Mahmud had heard and most of which he had not, the Hoca broke up the gathering, asking them all to come back the next morning and learn more of the sacred teachings of Mohammed. Some of these meetings were interesting even to small boys, as the Hoca would tell about the days when the Prophet had been a child, and how he had been orphaned at a very early age. After a short period of time, his grandfather, who had adopted him, also died. Then the young Prophet was adopted by his uncle who had taken Mohammed throughout Syria and Arabia with his camel caravans. Mahmud, who had been named after the Prophet, thought that it would be very exciting to go with a caravan, but he would be very frightened. Best of all, though, he liked to hear about the wars that were waged to establish the new religion and to drive the infidels out of Mecca. Sometimes the Hoca told exciting tales of the crusades, and how the heroic Moslem soldiers had driven out the invading unbelievers, but today he had talked only about the beliefs of the religion and the responsibilities of all good Moslems, which were very dull and uninteresting subjects to Mahmud. He listened a little, but mostly he thought about the wars, until the Hoca rose and said that the class was over.

10

The Turkish Bath

O<small>NE HOT</small> August morning Mahmud's father told him that they were going to the city to the *hamam* (turkish bath) and bathe so that they would be clean and ready to present their sacrifices to Allah on the following morning, which was the *Kurban* (sacrifice) *Bayram*. This holiday, along with others on the Moslem calendar, moves back ten days annually so that over a period of years it can occur at different seasons, and this year it was coming in the late summer.

The trips to the bath were very exciting for Mahmud, as for most Turkish boys, because it combined an outing with his father, a trip to the city, and a picnic of sorts. When he had been younger, he had gone occasionally to the women's *hamam* with his mother, but he had been allowed to go with his father to the men's *hamam* for the past few years. This was just one further sign that he was growing up.

While Mahmud stood talking with his father about the coming excursion, his mother came out of the house carrying a large basket filled with food that she had prepared for them to eat at the *hamam*. They would spend most of the day there and would be very hungry long before they were ready to return to the village that evening.

The basket contained five sheets of flat round *pide* (village bread), some fresh green grapes, white cheese, black olives, two cold eggplants stuffed with rice and oozing olive oil, and a small package of *helva* (a type of candy made of flour, sugar, and oil that comes in a variety of forms and is fairly common throughout the Middle East). In addition, the basket held the following items: two copper bowls (*tas*), some soap, two small glovelike washcloths of heavy canvas, and some turkish towels. These were the tools with which they would remove the accumulation of dirt from their bodies.

Taking the basket from his wife, Mahmud's father said goodbye to her and started off toward the city as the boy followed close behind him. It was a typical August morning in Anatolia. The sky was a clear brilliant blue as the sun hung in the eastern sky. Not a cloud could be seen, and since there had been no rain for almost two months, the greenness of the plants was dulled by the grayish dust that blew up at the slightest disturbance. This powder would then resettle on any and everything to give it a grayish lifeless caste. Despite all this, it was comfortable in the early morning air, because the altitude made for cool nights and it took some time for the sun to heat the air.

As they neared the city limits, they saw many others from different villages converging on the town. Some men and women brought produce to the city to sell, some came to shop in the markets, and many were, as Mahmud and his father, headed for the *hamam*. Movement into the city was always increased just before a Bayram. The city dwellers needed lambs to sacrifice and so they were willing to pay a higher price than usual for them. They also needed food for the meals celebrating the occasion, and the peasants required manufactured goods, such as material for new clothes, from the stores in the city.

Near the outer edge of the town was a very old building that had been there for centuries. It was hexagonal in shape and topped by a cluster of domes, perforated with a design of holes, which was intended to let light in and steam out at the same time. An accumulation of vegetation and debris had covered about one-third of the structure so that it appeared to be growing right out of the earth. Beneath the floor there were a series of coal fires that heated the water as it ran through tiles after having bubbled up out of a nearby spring. This heated water was then piped up to the main bathing area and allowed to run freely into several large stone sinks without drain pipes. The water simply ran over the edges of the basins, onto the floor, and out of the building.

Mahmud and his father were met at the door by an old man wearing only a pair of black trousers and wooden, thonglike shoes. He welcomed them, took their money, and led them along a narrow marble-lined hallway to a row of small wooden stalls wherein they could undress, hang their things on pegs that protruded from the walls, and leave their food and other belongings there while they were in the bath itself.

Undressing quickly, Mahmud and his father walked out of the little room, down another short marble-lined hallway that was damp with moisture but very clean, and out into a large open space bounded by six walls and covered by a cluster of domes. The larger of these was supported by six smaller ones, one resting on the top of each wall. Below each of these small domes, with one exception, was a marble bowl without a drain. Into these spilled two constant streams of water that came from pipes protruding from the walls just above them, and the excess water overflowed around the edges and fell to the floor where it disappeared into drains. On both sides of these were marble benches on which the bathers could sit. The air was filled with steam that swirled around just below the small circular holes in the ceiling as cold air tried to get in and warm steam out at the same time.

Passing several men already engaged in bathing, Mahmud and his father went over to an unoccupied basin and seated themselves on either side of it. Once in a comfortable position, Mahmud caught a little of the cold water in his *tas* (bowl), mixed some of the hot water with it, and poured the mixture over his body. Sitting silently as his father talked to him about things of interest to grownups but unintelligible to children, he poured one *tas* after another of water over himself, each one a little warmer than the last. This was accomplished by putting less cold and more hot water into the bowl each time so that the mixture was as hot as he could stand. The warmth relaxed him completely, except for the hand that poured the water, and he watched the steam swirl about in the air currents from the holes in the roof or listened to the talk, as suited his mood at the moment, because his father's remarks rarely required an answer anyway.

With each succeeding bowl his body grew redder and hotter until he was finally pouring the liquid directly from the hot pipe onto his body with no discomfort. Mahmud continued this operation until even the hot water seemed cool. Then his father, apparently also having finished with this phase, rose and started to walk toward two stone tables in a small alcove off the main room. A great deal of time had been passed in the preceding activity. It was past lunch time, and he and his father were both very red and hot when they reached two tables where an attendant appeared to be rubbing the dirt off one man by sheer force. Mahmud's father climbed up on the empty table that was unattended for the moment and waited for someone to come. Mahmud relaxed for a few minutes while the available attendant finished with the man he was working on, and then he climbed up and waited to be washed. Actually, washed was perhaps the wrong term for what happened. Perhaps scrubbed would be a better word for it, because the attendant grabbed his arm, took the *kese* (the canvas washcloth) that Mahmud carried in his *tas,* and began to rub the boy vigorously with it. As the rough canvas was pressed hard against the skin, large blackish beads of dirt began to form and fall off onto the floor as the attendant kept mumbling half to himself, *"çok pis, çok pis"* (very dirty).

Occasionally the attendant would throw a bowl of water over his victim to remove an accumulation of dirt so that he could continue. Mahmud felt as if the man were taking part of his skin off, which he may have been, despite his comments about the dirt. When the first arm was clean, Mahmud's assailant grabbed the other one, flipped him over as if he were a dead fish, and began to work on it. He and his father were both scrubbed all over, except on the face, the genitals, and the bottoms of their feet.

When the man appeared to be satisfied that he had scraped as much dirt off as was possible, he took the soap that Mahmud's father had been carefully protecting and sudsed the boy into a blob of froth before dousing him with warm water to wash away the soap as well as any specks of dirt that might still remain on his body after the rubbing operation. The water, soap, and all ran onto the marble paved floor and into the only drains in the room. When he was completely clean, including a thorough washing of his hair, Mahmud climbed off the table and waited for the man to finish with his father. By this time they were both exhausted and extremely hungry, so they walked very slowly toward the cubicle in which they had left their lunch basket. Once inside the small room they fell limply on the seat and just sat there for a few minutes. Then, with a great effort, Mahmud's father managed to open the basket and draw out some food for them to eat.

Along the sides of the dressing area were two boards covered with turkish towels on which they could rest. They ate very slowly, but managed to consume all that the basket contained and wished that there had been more in it. They then lay down to rest, and spent the better part of the afternoon lying down. However, sometime before the sun touched the horizon, they had regained enough strength to get up and start homeward, despite the fact that the walk seemed long in their half-exhausted state. Mahmud concluded that bathing was an experience that he would not want to repeat too often, but now he was clean enough for the Bayram that would come the next day.

11

The Kurban Bayram

HE NEXT MORNING Mahmud rose to greet another typical Anatolian summer day, slipped on his outer garments, and ate his usual breakfast of white cheese, bread, and olives with a cup of hot tea. After eating he went with his father some distance from the village to the sheep pens. These structures were mostly for lambing, but could be utilized at any time if it were necessary to keep the sheep corralled. The pens were circular pits, which were dug into the earth about three feet and extended above the ground level by a wall made simply of loose stones piled in a circle. An entry could be effected through a break in the crude fence, which had been left at the top of a steeply inclined ramp. When Mahmud and his father arrived, the gate was closed by a huge boulder, as it always was when the pens were occupied. The boy attempted to move the rock alone, but it was far too heavy for him and the man had to push it aside.

Mahmud's father looked over the half-dozen sheep in this pen, selected the one that he thought would provide the best meat for this very special occasion, the Kurban Bayram, and pointed it out to his son. The boy set about immediately to catch the animal and with a little help he soon held it firmly, but gently, against one wall of the enclosure. A rope was fastened securely about its neck, and they started back toward the edge of the village, leaving the other sheep free to go about their business.

As the two men walked they met others who were coming from their homes bound for their own sheep-pens. Normal pleasantries were exchanged as the celebrants passed each other, and occasionally they would pause to discuss the coming day with one of their neighbors. Considerable time had elapsed before they reached the spot just outside the village where they were to kill the lamb, and the sun was about halfway up in the morning sky. Just as they arrived the call for prayer sounded from the mosque, and this being a holy day, there was nothing to be done but render the appropriate sacrament. Mahmud held the sheep and tried to keep it quiet while his father faced toward the southeast and laid out a prayer rug, which he often carried with him when he knew that he would be away from home at these important times. Kneeling and removing his shoes, he took some water from a small earthenware jug, which had been left there to rinse off the knife after the slaughter of the lamb, and symbolically washed his hands, feet, and face, paying special attention to his eyes, nose, mouth, and ears. Then Mahmud watched as his father mumbled the prayers in Arabic, shifting his position frequently, making strange movements with his hands, and touching his forehead to the ground at intervals. The boy watched for several minutes and tried to remember as much of these movements as he could, because he knew that in years to come it would be necessary for him to pray, and each movement and intonation of the prayer had a special meaning.

When Mahmud's father had finished praying, he came over to where the boy was standing. Mahmud held the rope as his father took a knife from his belt and straddled the tethered animal. The sharp blade was carefully placed over a ritually sanctioned spot on the sheep's throat, and Mahmud's father said a short prayer and severed the great arteries with a single quick stroke. For an instant life seemed to flicker in the animal's eyes, and then it was all over. Thus they had rendered unto God the sacrifice, as Abraham had done so long ago as a substitute for his son, that was now required annually of all good Moslems.

The animal jerked a few times and then lay still. It was allowed to bleed freely for a long while before Mahmud's father opened the abdomen, removed the entrails, piled them high on a piece of heavy canvas, and began to carve up the carcass. Some of the meat was carried by Mahmud to relatives who were in need, but most of it was taken home where his mother and the new *gelin* were already preparing a huge feast for the evening meal.

Just before noon Mahmud went with his father to the mosque. After leaving their shoes outside the door, they walked toward the Hoca who sat cross-legged in front of the worship area, ready to begin the services. Mahmud's father turned the bill of his cap around to the back of his head, and he and his son both kneeled down on the floor. The Hoca waited a few minutes as others came in and seated themselves in a similar manner. Then, turning toward Mecca, he began to chant in Arabic. The kneeling men listened until the leader stopped, and then they repeated what he had said. The Hoca chanted another short verse, and the men again repeated it. This continued for some time, and at odd intervals, which Mahmud did not understand, the entire group touched their heads to the floor. Mahmud watched his father and tried to follow his movements exactly, though he knew that he could not say the prayers correctly. Thus, the boy took still another step along the pathway to manhood.

After about an hour of praying in the manner described above, the Hoca rose, walked to a small platform at the top of the stairway in the right-hand corner of the front of the mosque and seated himself cross-legged again. There he gave a long lecture on the virtues of the Moslem religion, exhorting the men to live virtuous lives and to see to it that their families followed the words of the prophet so that they would always live as Mohammed had taught them. References were occasionally made to the decay that had set in in the religious life of the country in the past few years and how they should resist such changes. The Hoca pleaded with them all to try to return their village to the way of life that had been in style at the time of Mohammed (Arabia, 570 to 632 AD), to remember the teachings of the Koran, and to be guided in all things by these divine words. Then the gathering broke up, and all went their separate ways, each heading toward his own home to partake of the noonday meal.

That afternoon was not very different from other afternoons, except that no one worked in the fields. The women were busy preparing the large meals that would be eaten that evening, and the men sat in the shade of the houses or under a tree and talked. The children were decked out in their Sunday best, but played about the town pretty much as usual.

In every home that could afford it there was to be a huge feast that night, usually attended by some of the poorer relatives. Mahmud's family was no exception, and when the evening prayers were past, aunts and uncles began to arrive. Soon the men were seated about the small circular table in the men's living room chatting idly and waiting to be served. First a large bowl of *etli fasulye* (a thin broth containing beans with small chunks of lamb) was brought in from the kitchen by Mahmud. When all had had their fill of this, a great bowl of *iç pilav* (rice with pine nuts and a variety of seasonings) was brought out. Then came a tray piled high with *lahmacun dolması* (a meat and rice mixture wrapped in cabbage leaves). A short time later this near-empty tray was taken away and replaced by one filled with *börek* (ground meat or cheese wrapped in thin dough and fried). Then a dish of tomatoes and cucumbers with olive oil and vinegar was put on the table for the men to munch on while the dessert, *kadayif* (a pastry saturated with sugar water), was prepared. After this had been brought out and eaten, a tray filled with apples, grapes, oranges, apricots, and tangerines, most of which had been bought in the nearby city, was placed on the table. The men sat in the dim light of the small electric bulb for a long time that night, discussing both religious and political issues and nibbling at the fruit. In the meantime the women ate in the other room, cleaned up the dishes, and stored away the leftovers for a future meal. Mahmud had eaten far too much that evening and went to bed with a stomach ache, a sensation which would be gone and forgotten by the time he awoke the next morning.

12

The Ramazan

THE WINTER PASSED as usual, and finally, near spring, came the long month of Ramazan. Each morning, long before sunrise, the boom of a cannon that was fired in the nearby city was heard in the village, and everyone got up quickly. The women in Mahmud's household took loaves of bread, fresh fruits, and vegetables from the storage room and warmed over the heavy meal from the evening before. Everyone ate heartily at breakfast time, because they were storing up for the long day without food or water. All ate rapidly, for it was necessary to finish eating before sunup, at which time a second cannon was fired. This was to tell everyone that he should eat no more until the firing of still a third cannon some time after sunset that evening. For the adults who had been through many fasts going without food was not much of a hardship, but for Mahmud, who had never really fasted before, it was very difficult. However, he had to do it, and somehow he managed to live, though he thought at times that his stomach would surely digest itself.

During the daytime work went on as usual. The women prepared food, and the men did whatever they deemed important and worth doing. If it were unusually hot in the afternoon, they would go to the grove of poplars outside the village, sit in the shade, and discuss the affairs of the community and country. The children played and were hungry.

Finally darkness came and everyone went home, because when the cannon fired again, they could break their fast. This they did with a vengeance. The women prepared a huge meal, and everyone, being very hungry, stuffed themselves. They probably ate more during the fast than during the rest of the year.

The Ramazan lasted for a full month, then came a three-day period usually referred to as the *Şeker Bayram,* though actually only the first day was the Bayram (sugar or candy holiday). This day, the breaking of the month of fast, was set aside for feasting and celebration. After a regular breakfast all the children were taken to see their grandparents where they would first kiss the backs of the hands of the old folks and touch the spot that had been kissed to their foreheads. The old people would offer the children candy and sometimes gifts. They would then go on to visit other relatives and repeat this same procedure. The entire three-day period was one of visiting and gossiping, but not working. Many of the men went to the mosque on the day of the Şeker Bayram to say special prayers or to hear a sermon by the Hoca, but many did not.

$$\boxed{13}$$

A Birth and a Death

NE FINAL SCENE before we leave Mahmud to continue his life in Anatolia as his ancestors have in centuries past. His lot may be a little different, however. New influences are subtly affecting his way of life, and perhaps by the time his son sits, as Mahmud does now, high on the hill far away from the village, surveying the landscape below him, things will be very different.

Eight to ten thousand years ago agriculture was discovered in the Middle East. Following this discovery there was a rapid rise in the cultural standards of the area, a coalescing of village culture, and then a long period of more or less static life. This is not to say that there were no changes during this time, for there were many, but mostly the advances affected the cities of the area, not the village dwellers. Century after century the peasants have tilled their land with oxen and a wooden plow, ground their bread with a crude millstone, and reared their children in the time-honored manner. Even during the first half of the twentieth century most of the villagers lived in what could best be described as a cultural level very similar to the early iron age. Only in the late 1950s did this begin to change perceptibly.

One overlord replaced another throughout the centuries and taxes were paid to different rulers, but otherwise the villager's lot was unchanged; centered as it was in the things that occupied the lives of the small farming communities. Such things as births, marriages, circumcisions, deaths, tilling the soil, and harvesting the crops were of greatest importance.

With the coming of Atatürk in the early 1920s, a profound change began, which has not as yet reached its climax. Even in 1962 many villages were just beginning to really feel the effects of Atatürk's revolution, and with the new modes of communication and transportation, compulsory education, and the central government's emphasis on modernity, the older way of life will probably pass away and be forgotten in a few decades, despite its long history.

Mahmud feels the stirrings of this new era, an era of democracy, freedom, and a new way of life for him and his friends in the village; all of the boys, and many of the girls, are now going to school; prices improve with each passing year, and more and better consumer goods appear in the village homes. Mahmud does not, of course, comprehend these things or their implications for the future.

As Mahmud sits on his lonely hilltop, not far above the village, he can see two scenes below, both of which he knows something about, yet he understands neither. Near one house, very much like his own, there is a flurry of activity as the older women in the village scurry about bringing hot water and the like to the young woman within, who is trying desperately to give birth to a child that does not seem to want to enter this world. Mahmud watches this for a while and knows that as soon as the child is born it will be wrapped tightly in clean, pure white cloth. Later, a small blue bead will be pinned onto the swaddling clothes to protect the child from the evil eye. Soon thereafter everyone in the village will be invited to come and see the new arrival. When they come, each one will be offered a sweet beverage to drink, and each one will say "maşallah" and immediately thereafter make some comment about the child's beauty, strength, or intelligent expression. Finally, after a short visit, during which some small gift might or might not be left for the baby, they will say goodbye and go back to their own homes. Many other things of importance will happen to the mother and child, but Mahmud does not know about these things, partially because he is a child, and partially because he is male. Anyway, he does not find the birth of babies of particular consequence to him.

Turning his head to the right, he can also see a house where an old man has died. Here again he does not know too much about what happens during the preparations for burial immediately after death, except what he can observe from his vantage point. He is old enough now to wonder about what happens to people when they die, but he does not really know, and he wonders also whether the old folks know or not. They always tell him that he will go to heaven, but he does not understand this either.

As Mahmud contemplates these things, he can see a group of men gather around the door of the house. Then a plain wooden box, which contains the body of the deceased, seems to float out the door above the heads of the milling throng of men. This illusion is the result of an attempt by everyone to help lift the coffin. As soon as it is out of the door, the group makes its way slowly toward the village mosque. As they move, the casket still appears to float about above the men on a sea of hands and arms. Each person believes that it is an honor, indeed a religious obligation, to help carry the coffin during a part of the trip to its final resting place.

Toward the end of this cluster of men, strung out irregularly in its movements down the village street, Mahmud can see an old man who is walking with tears in his downcast eyes. Two younger men are hitting this pathetic creature with their fists and teasing him. This sight saddens Mahmud somewhat, yet he knows that this must always be so. Those who mourn have to be teased and kept constantly thinking of things other than death, lest they lose their minds completely. This idea is so strong among Turks that they have an expression, *"Başınıza sag olsun,"* which means, "Let your head (mind) be healthy." This is repeated to anyone who has just lost a relative or close friend.

As Mahmud watches, the crowd reaches the mosque and goes inside the wall around the building. The Hoca comes out and says a short prayer over the coffin, and then goes with the people to the small graveyard some distance from the village. This area looks like a field of stones, not the finely polished marble monuments that one usually associates with cemeteries, but simply rough stones that are shaped like irregular rectangles, very thin, with no markings to indicate who lies beneath them. Each grave is covered with a heap of small rocks in the general shape of a rectangle. The head of each grave is marked by a large stone shaped in the manner described above and the foot of the grave by a smaller stone.

An uneven rectangular hole, about three feet deep, had been dug that morning, and the body is removed from the casket and lowered immediately into it. Then the Hoca reads a rather lengthy passage from the Koran, and the dirt is filled in. Finally, the rocks are placed above the grave, and the group of men disperse, each going back to his own home. This leaves only the old man. He stands alone beside the grave of his brother, who had been the last living member of the old man's immediate family. Now there were no old relatives left in his family, only the children and their children. The old man stands silently, his head bowed slightly, for a long period of time. Finally, he too turns and trudges wearily back toward the village, leaving his dead brother in the hands of Allah.

Mahmud does not understand what he sees, and he cannot know the old man's emotions, but he feels sorry for anyone who looks so very sad. Glancing back toward the small cluster of earth-colored houses, he realizes that the village population remained the same, as one person had come into the world and another had gone out of it. He understands in a vague way that some day he would go to make room for someone else, but for the first time in his life it occurs to him that someday his mother and father would be called away, and this thought makes him feel terribly sad. This too is a part of his growing up, a very painful part, but one which he could not escape. All of this, he had been taught, is a part of Allah's plans for the world. Neither he nor anyone else would ever completely understand this plan, but everyone should try to bend his life to be a part of it. Nothing could be accomplished in this world without the sanction of Allah.

Looking out over the bright clear landscape, Mahmud sees only peace and tranquility. Here and there below him are men following their oxen as they till the land. A few children walk slowly to or from the fountain to fetch water for their mothers, and the gentle wind pushes soft clouds across the endless stretch of blue above him. Mahmud is impressed by the vastness of the world about him, but he has no inkling of the infinite variety and complexity that exists beyond what he can see.

Thoughts of death draw a darkening, invisible pall over this scene of beauty that spreads out below him and Mahmud is sad. This awareness of death as an inevitable part of life is the final sign that he is becoming a man. Many fears will plague him during his adolescent years, and perhaps even more when he is full grown, but he can not avoid these things anymore than he can avoid death.

Dropping his head down on his arms, he sits with a heavy heart as he looks into the future to a time when his father and mother would surely die, leaving him a small plot of land to till and a family of his own. Despite the things that he had been taught in school, he thinks of life only in terms of tilling his father's land, marrying a girl from the village, and rearing his own children as he had been reared. No one can know at this point whether these things will come to pass or not, but it is unlikely, for Mahmud is good in his classes at school and things are changing. Perhaps he will become a doctor, a teacher, or something that he has not even heard of as yet.

PART TWO

A Partial Ethnography

14

The Village of Demirciler

AHMUD'S VILLAGE is in many respects typical of the villages in Central Anatolia. Anadolu, as the Turks call Anatolia, is what Americans are used to thinking of as Asia Minor. Central Anatolia is a semi-arid plateau above 2000 feet in elevation. The region is bounded on all sides by mountains, some of which reach elevations in excess of 12,000 feet; high enough to screen most of the moisture from the air.

The Anatolian Turk is Caucasoid with some Mongoloid admixture, but the residents of Demirciler show no Mongoloid traits. They seem to be racially related to the Europeans in northwestern Greece. Their skin is quite light, except where suntanned. They have dark brown eyes and dark brown to black hair. Many older males grow fairly heavy mustaches, and in general the men appear to be moderately hairy. They are medium in stature, males averaging about five foot seven inches, I would estimate, since actual measurements were not made. The men have muscular bodies, even the older ones. It is difficult to describe the women from appearances because they wore three or four layers of heavy clothing. One day my wife asked a woman from one of the villages near Ankara to take off her clothes and weigh herself on our bathroom scale; she weighed about 132 pounds. She was over 40 years old. Incidentally, she appeared to weigh about 160 pounds with her clothes on.

Central Anatolia is very sparsely settled. As a matter of fact, one can drive for hours in some regions and see hardly any signs of human life. This is perhaps the most primitive area in Turkey, as it has, until very recently, been effectively cut off from communication with the outside world by the mountains surrounding it. The central plateau is much less productive than the rest of Turkey, though it has considerable potential for large-scale production of small grains if machines become available.

Mahmud's village, Demirciler, is near the city of Kaman, approximately 110 kilometers southeast of Ankara on the road to Kayseri. It is not directly on the highway. In 1961 one had to turn off just before entering Kaman and drive on a small oxcart trail for about two kilometers up the side of a fairly sharply rising hillside to reach the sprawling, irregular cluster of stone and mud-brick houses.

The village consists of some 50 families who occupy independent dwelling units. These vary in size from a simple nuclear family—mother, father, and children—to extended families consisting of an elderly couple with two or three married sons and their children, all living under a single roof. In 1950, according to my principal informant, there had been only 15 houses in the village. The growth from 15 to about 50 houses in this village is unusual, but it is indicative of the general population explosion occurring throughout Turkey. However, the village's growth has been accelerated due to the following factors: (1) its nearness to Kaman and the highway to Ankara have given the villagers a steadily growing, easily accessible market for their product; (2) the introduction of the steel-turning plow has enabled the villagers to produce larger surpluses than they were able to with the traditional wooden ones. Further, the nearness of Kaman gave them access to a good school and medical facilities that are not available to most Anatolian villages.

Standing on the highway some two kilometers away from Demirciler and looking up toward the village one sees nothing very different from what might be seen by looking at hundreds of other villages scattered about Anatolia. From a distance most of the houses can hardly be seen as they are the same color and general texture as the earth from which they were made, though a few have some whitewash on the outer walls as a result of the improved economy. There is no plan for the village. The houses seem to be oriented in any way that suited the builder, and the only hint of streets are rough, winding trails that simply fill the spaces between the houses.

The only building in the village that has a tile roof is the new mosque, which, as a matter of fact, was said to be only about ten years old in 1961. Nearly all the homes are rectangular in shape, one-story structures, cut from a common floor plan, with flat mud roofs that have a large white stone-roller on top to press the roofing materials after heavy rains. Precipitation is rare, but does occur in late winter and early spring, occasionally with disastrous results. One woman who worked in Ankara did not show up one day. She explained later that her house had "melted" in the heavy rains, and that she had been busy helping her sons put the walls back up. The mean annual rainfall in this area is only slightly over ten inches, but much of this occurs in heavy cloudbursts in the early spring. The summer sky is typically cloudless, the air clear and bright, and the days hot with fairly cold nights, even in July and August.

Near the center of the village is a fountain with four iron spouts from which water runs continuously. This is the water supply for the entire village. The young girls carry all of the water for cooking, washing, and so forth to the houses in earthenware and copper pots that are purchased from the nearby city, and the laundry is done at the site of the spring. Almost every morning a small group of women can be seen, each with a pile of clothes and a large copper pot, gossiping and doing the weekly wash on the stone platform onto which the water from the spouts falls. The Menderes government had run a new water line from a source in the mountains to a reservoir on the hill just above the village. This supplemented the water supply for Kaman, and the government had promised to pipe water into the village homes soon. However, with the change in governments and the execution of Menderes in 1962, this may be a long time in coming.

Many homes in the village have electricity, which according to the informants, was installed in 1958. This is a convenience of dubious value, however, as current is available only between six and ten o'clock in the evening. Several houses have a single strand of wire hanging from the ceiling of some of the larger rooms and this provides current for a very small bulb. Some houses have a single wall plug, but there are no appliances to plug into the outlet.

Looking away from the village toward the west, one can see for a great distance an uneven landscape of gently rolling hills. The general appearance of these hills is a dull gray, except for a few weeks in April and May when spring grasses color it green. The valleys are green in spring from young wheat and golden after the end of June from the ripened stalks of grain. The plots in these valleys are each cultivated by a single man with a team of oxen to provide wheat for his family and a small surplus to sell. There are also small groves of trees scattered here and there. These have grown up around some source of water. Beneath the foliage, where there is a large enough surplus of freely flowing water, irrigated vegetable gardens provide the villagers with tomatoes, peppers, eggplant, squash, and a few other vegetables.

The relationship of man to his environment has for centuries been colored by the need for water in this area. Wherever water is found there is rich green vegetation, but where there is none the rocky surface of the hills produces only a scanty growth of tough grass on which the hardy fat-tailed sheep and goats of the area can survive.

The villagers depend principally on agriculture and herding for their livelihood. Surpluses of grain are sold to the wheat bank, and sheep, goats, and vegetable surpluses are sold in Kaman for cash with which the manufactured goods needed can be purchased. The only wildlife observed about the village consisted of storks, which the peasants believed to be good omens and refused to kill, and several varieties of small birds. There are wolves and wild boars reported back in the mountains.

The basis of subsistence is wheat farming. Each adult male tills a plot of land as large as he can manage, since all of the villagers own more land than they can till at one time. Until very recently this was done with a wooden plow, but in 1961 small steel turning plows had replaced most of the more primitive implements. These steel plows have only about a four-inch turning blade and are for the most part still pulled by teams of oxen, though occasionally horses are used. However, most peasants still use wooden plows in other Anatolian villages, and since the land is stony and not too fertile, this is strenuous work. The land must be plowed and the rocks taken out of the field and piled nearby, and this process must be repeated several times until the ground is comparatively free of stones. Then a crude harrow, consisting only of a single log, attached at a 90° angle to a pole that is then yoked to a team of oxen, or occasionally horses, is dragged over the land to break up the clods. Finally, the grain is sown by hand and the harrow dragged once more over the field to cover the seeds with earth.

When the wheat is fully mature, it is cut by grasping it in the left hand and cutting a handful at a time with a small hand sickle held in the right hand. The cut stalks are then raked into piles with a wooden rake, consisting of a handle with a wooden crosspiece on one end about 2 by 2 by 30 inches with round pegs about 3 inches apart and 4 inches long acting as raking prongs. The piles of cut wheat remain on the ground until the entire field has been cut. The stacks are then loaded onto 2-wheeled oxcarts equipped with a special hay-frame, made by attaching 2 long poles to the center of the back of the cart to make a "v," which is then raised toward the front of the wagon and supported by two shorter poles, about 4 feet long, that slope obliquely up from the two front corners of the cart's main bed. The wheat is hauled in this cart to the threshing floor, which may be quite some distance from the field. Here the wheat is spread out on the hard surface and threshed by running over it a flat board, which is turned up at the front so that it looks much like a short tobog-gan. Sharp flakes of flint or obsidian are imbedded in the bottom of the threshing sled to make an efficient cutting device for separating the grain from its husk. This device is pulled by oxen, for the most part, though sometimes it is pulled by horses, tractors (rented from Kaman, but not often), or even donkeys. After the grain is separated from the husks, the mixture is raked into a pile in the center of the circular threshing floor and winnowed by throwing the grain and chaff into the air with a wooden, cylindrical container about 18 inches in diameter and four inches deep with a wire screen bottom. The straw and chaff are utilized in many ways, including feed for donkeys, sheep, goats, and cattle; building materials, when mixed with earth; and fuel, when mixed with dung. The grain is then spread out on a large cloth to dry and bagged and stored for later use.

As it is needed, the grain is taken to a water-driven mill and ground. The mill is constructed of two horizontal stones, one above the other. The lower millstone is held firmly in place, with a rotating shaft running through a hole in the center of it. The upper stone is attached to this shaft and turns from the power of water forced horizontally from a funnel-shaped, hollowed log that stands almost upright, gathering water from a spring at a higher elevation. Wheat is fed into a small hole in the center of the upper stone and ground as this stone revolves. The ground flour works its way out to the edges and accumu-lates in small piles around the edges of the mill. The flour is then swept up, put into large white bags, and taken back to the village where it is stored until it is needed. About once every three months a large number of women get together and mix up a batch of bread dough. They then spend the entire day rolling out sheets of dough about 20 inches in diameter and an eighth of an inch thick. These are baked on top of a convex, circular sheet of iron that covers a subterranean fireplace. When the day is over, each family has two or three piles of sheets of tough, leathery bread; each pile being about a meter in height. This is not only tasty but very nutritious and will last the family for about three months at which time another baking "bee" is held.

These sheets of bread are unleavened and serve very nicely for making spoons, or perhaps more properly scoops, with which one can eat the many kinds of stew made by the villagers. You tear a small piece of bread from one of the sheets and, by deftly folding it in your fingers, make a small scoop that holds about a tablespoon of food. Then one dips this into the dish and eats both spoon and food.

Much of the subsistence of the village also comes from sheep and goats. These animals feed on the sparse grasses in the hills and are slaughtered for food, sheared for wool, and sold for cash. A shepherd comes to the village each morning and collects all of the sheep. These are grazed during the day on land that it held in common by the villagers and called empty land. No one can break this land for farming under any circumstances, so they say. It will be interesting to see if this prohibition will hold up when the current crop of children grow up, and there is not enough farm land to go aronnd.

Each evening the animals are brought back to the village. The shepherd is paid for his work at sporadic intervals by gifts of animals or money by the villagers. This man does not belong either to the village or to Kaman; he lives alone back in the mountains. The peasants do not eat much meat, but occasionally for weddings, guests, or special occasions an animal is slaughtered. There is no way of preserving meat, other than just cooking up large batches of whatever one wishes to make and then reheating it every day until it is all eaten. A common way of cooking an animal is to roast it whole in a large communal oven. A mixture of vegetables with a little meat in water is common, as are a variety of rice dishes seasoned with small quantities of meat. The rice is not raised in the village; it is bought for cash in Kaman, as are the many seasonings used in cooking, along with some fruits and vegetables that they do not grow. Grapes, melons, and some vegetables are grown in irrigated gardens and surpluses are sold in Kaman. The vegetables that are not raised in the village are brought into Kaman by truck from the south.

The irrigation systems are fairly complicated, consisting of ditches, raised aqueducts, made from earth, and hollowed half-logs that serve to carry the water across gullies. The water flows continuously out of springs here and there, and this flow is utilized constantly. The water is diverted to one field or another by blocking one channel with mud and opening another. Very little of this precious water is wasted. When one plot has had sufficient water, the stream is blocked and another channel opened, allowing the water to flow to a dry field. Demirciler is more fortunate than most in having much more available water.

Thick thread is spun from the wool of the sheep and goats. A large ball of wool is held in the left hand and attached to a wooden whorl, a long thin stick slightly enlarged in the middle, which is given a quick twist with the right hand and allowed to hang free. The movement causes the whorl to spin and wool is fed out evenly as the spinning whorl drops toward the ground. This pendulum arrangement is kept swinging back and forth and is allowed to strike the upper part of the thigh on each pass, maintaining the spin. When the whorl gets almost to the ground, the thread is wound around it and the process repeated. This thread is then dyed and used to make heavy woolen vests, socks, and carpeting. Heavy bolsters, handbags, and bags for carrying heavy items on the back of a donkey are all made from this material as are the rugs on the floors of the village homes.

Other animals of great importance are water buffalo, which serve as draft animals and provide meat as well as milk products, and the donkey which carries the villager and his produce wherever he wants to go. A considerable amount of cheese, a beverage similar to buttermilk called *ayran*, and butter are made from milk and used, but not sold, by the villagers. The fresh milk is boiled immediately after milking and poured into a calf-skin supported by a wooden frame about six feet high. This skin sweats, keeping the contents cool. The milk sours as it is kept here and preserved until it is needed, when it is taken out to make cheese, *ayran*, and butter.

Four men in the village draw cash incomes from the central government: the Muhtar (headman), the Hoca (Moslem minister), the village Bekçi (watchman), and the field Bekçi. The Muhtar is responsible for recording births, deaths, and marriages; collecting taxes; selecting men for the army each year; and entertaining visitors. The Hoca is responsible for the spiritual life of the village and care of the mosque. The village Bekçi is responsible for maintaining the peace, and if someone gets too unruly he calls on the Jandarma (national internal security forces). The field Bekçi keeps animals from the fields. All of these men, except the Hoca, are elected.

The village was in the recent past economically almost self-sufficient. It could probably be so again should the situation require it in the near future, as most of the old people know how to make nearly everything that they need, except iron tools, but presently Demirciler is being rapidly integrated into the national economy of Turkey. This means a money economy with an increasing quantity of cotton cloth, kerosene, and other manufactured items being brought in from the outside each year in exchange for the ever larger surpluses of wheat, vegetables, and wool. Cotton cloth is rapidly replacing much of the woolen clothing, and kerosene is replacing the old fuel made of collected dung mixed with straw and water in the shape of pancakes that are burnable when dried. Some items such as Western type wooden tables and chairs are new additions.

The rapid growth of the population in the village has not as yet changed the basis of the economy, because most of the young people have not reached adulthood. The fact that the traditional economy will not be able to absorb all of the young men, coupled with the increased educational opportunity for the children, will probably mean that in the near future some young husbands will be taking jobs in Kaman and earning only cash incomes. Then what remains of the traditional way of life will begin to fade away quite rapidly.

The children in 1961 were all walking the two kilometers to the new government school on the outskirts of Kaman, or at least most of them were. In view of these developments Demirciler probably faces rapid changes similar to those described for the village of Balgat by Daniel Lerner in *The Passing of Traditional Society* (1958). In 1961 I visited Balgat and found it a thriving suburb of Ankara, with bus service to the city every 20 minutes; a superhighway running along one side; and a modern shopping center, sporting radios, electric toasters, and so on. Quite a change from the small, culturally isolated village first visited by Lerner in 1949.

15

The Turkish Language and Culture

A BRIEF SKETCH of some of the distinctive characteristics of standard Turkish and Turkic languages in general will be given below. Turkish is a member of the Turko-Tatar family, which belongs to the Ural-Altaic stock. This means that Turkish is remotely related to Finnish and Hungarian, as well as an array of languages spread all across Siberia. Actually, I used the standard Turkish to communicate with the villagers and noted only phonological differences between their speech and mine (for example, they frequently substituted a *g* for *k*, *Gonya* for *Konya*). I do not include notation of any of the dialectical differences that characterize the speech of the people in Demirciler in the sketch of standard Turkish given below.

The phonological system of Turkish consists of the following vowel phonemes:

	Rounded		Unrounded	
	Front	Back	Front	Back
High	*ü*	*u*	*i*	*ı*
Low	*ö*	*o*	*e*	*a*

Possibly *â*

The Turkish consonantal system is as follows:

p		*t*	*ç*	*k*
b		*d*	*c*	*g*
	f	*s*	*ş*	
	v	*z*	*j*	
		r		
		l		
m		*n*		
			y	*h*

Possibly *kʸ*, *gʸ*, *lʸ*

71

One of the most interesting phonological characteristics of Turkish is vowel harmony. This is a system wherein the last vowel in the stem or root of a word determines the vowels in the affixes that follow. For example, one set of affixes are such that if the last stem vowel is any front vowel, *i.e.,* vowels produced with the front of the tongue raised in the front of the mouth—*i, e, ö,* or *ü,* the affix vowel will be an *e,* but if the last stem vowel is a back vowel, *i.e.,* a sound produced with the back of the tongue raised in the back of the mouth—*ı, a, o,* or *u,* the affix will contain an *a:*

ev	house	*at*	horse
eve	to the house	*ata*	to the horse
ip	thread	*ot*	hay
ipte	in the thread	*otta*	in the hay

There are several complications to this oversimplified presentation, but this should show how one variety of vowel harmony works. There are also other types that I will not go into here. Vowel harmony is very important in Turkish because the language is one that utilizes a large number of affixes attached to a single stem to express concepts that would be expressed in English by a long sequence of separate words.

Consider the following set of examples:

ev	house
evler	houses
evleri	the houses (accusative)
evlerinde	in the houses
evlerindeki	the one who is in the houses
evlerindekiler	the ones who are in the houses
evlerindekilerle	with the ones who are in the houses

ufak	small
ufaklık	small change (money)
ufaklamak	to reduce in size
ufaklanmak	to shrink (passive voice)
ufaltmak	to cause to get smaller
ufarak	tiny

git	go
gitmek	to go
gider	he goes
giderim	I go
gidiyorum	I am going
gideceğim	I will go
gidecektim	I intended to go

The examples given above are meant only to illustrate the various ways in which Turkish combines strings of affixes attached to a single stem where English would utilize a string of independent words for the same meaning.

Turkish is then a language that uses fairly long words each composed of a string of meaningful parts tightly bound together, as indicated by the fact that the vowels in the stem determine the vowels in the affixes. One might say that the Turk considers the concepts labeled by such complex words as units whereas English speakers think of them as combinations of units.

A very common sentence type for Turkish consists of a time word, the subject, direct object, and verb in that order.

> *Yarm, Ahmet ekmeği getirecek.*
> Tomorrow, Ahmet bread will bring.

The verb generally comes at the end of a sentence with the nouns coming between the subject and the verb itself. Turkish has a neat system for making complex verbal statements by stringing verbs one after the other, each with a specific affixe attached to it. One example will suffice to illustrate the system.

kalkmak (stem *kalk*)	to get up
gitmek (stem *git*)	to go
-ip	just preceding
-ti	he, past tense
Kalkip gitti.	
He got up and left. (This indicates that the act of getting up immediately preceded the act of leaving.)	

Turkish grammar is extremely complicated, as one can see even from the few examples given above, but it is compartively consistent, which compensates somewhat for its complexity. The examples below show how a single stem *göz* (eye) forms the base for a large number of words with different, but related, meanings.

göz	eye
gözlük	glasses
gözlükcü	optometrist
gözlükcülük	optometry
gözlemek	to watch
gözükmek	to appear
gözetmek	to look after

Since some linguists feel that one's perception of the world about him is conditioned by the grammatical structure of his language, it would seem that the Turk should make a sharp distinction between things and qualities on the one hand and actions on the other, but would not differentiate so sharply between qualities and things. This is exemplified by the fact that in Turkish nouns include nearly all of what English speakers would call nouns, adjectives, and adverbs. Nouns can be made into verbs and verbs into nouns by derivation, but almost never does one find nouns used as verbs or verbs used as nouns without derivation. English on the other hand has hundreds of nouns such as walk, talk, table, and others that can be used as verbs as easily as nouns, indicating that speakers of English do not make such a sharp distinction between things and actions as the Turks do.

The linguistic structure further indicates that nouns in relation to actions occur in five states: (1) they are performing the action (subject or uninflected form); (2) the action is being done to them (accusative case); (3) something is moving toward the noun in time or space (dative case); (4) something is moving away from the noun in time or space (ablative); (5) the thing is occurring in the same dimension as some other thing.

The definitive nominal paradigm (that is the set of affixes that can be affixed to all nouns and only to nouns) is:

ev	subject	house
evi	accusative	the house (object)
eve	dative	to the house
evde	locative	at the house
evden	ablative	from the house

Any noun occurring in a sentence must be in one of the above forms. This means, if the language indeed reflects a cultural world view, that the Turks think automatically in these categories. The grammatical structure of their language leaves them no other alternative and a speaker cannot use a noun without putting it into one of these dimensions.

The verbal structure contains the following tense structures:

git	imperative	go
gider	aorist	he goes
gidecek	future	he will go
gitti	past	he went
gitmiş	-*miş* tense	he has/is gone
gidiyor	progressive	he is going

(perhaps strictly speaking not a tense, but an aspect)

In contrast with English, where some tense is automatically expressed by the verb form, whether time is relevant or not, Turkish has two "tenses" that are essentially time free, the -*miş* tense and aorist. The form *yanmış* is usually translated as "it has burned" but Turks squeal "*yanmış*" as they are being burned when one would expect them to say *yandi*, it burned; *yanar*, it burns; or *yaniyor*, it is burning. The aorist tense is time free, because it indicates that an action is repeated over a period of time, but this is not necessarily connected with the present. For example, *okula gider* means he goes to school, but -*er* can be used in the past as well as in the present time, as in *giderdi* (*git* to go, -*er* aorist tense marker, and -*di* past tense marker) he used to go to school.

Some, but not all, combinations of the above tenses are possible to express various meanings.

giderdi	he used to go	(at some indefinite time in the past he went repeatedly)
gidecekti	he intended to go	(at some time in the past he was going to go at some future time)

Further, unlike English, wherein the perfect tenses are concerned with the time of completion of actions, Turkish cannot easily express forms such as: "We will have finished by eight o'clock." This is not meant to imply that English is more expressive than Turkish, but only that with the English structure goes a preoccupation with the relationship of times of actions, and the Turk is not limited or constrained by his language structure to always express the relationship of actions to time when this relationship is not important, whereas the English speaker is so constrained.

I feel that Turks are not nearly as concerned with the termination of actions as English speakers are, and perhaps this is a result of the Turkish linguistic structure. In working on several projects involving high officials in the Turkish government, I found it very difficult to get them to concern themselves seriously with a termination date for a particular job. Termination dates proposed were frequently not thought out at all and quite erratically determined. Then any statement concerned with the termination was always preceded by "*Inşallah*" (if it fits God's plan), and in most cases things were then allowed to drift as if God were controlling the work so why should they worry.

One negative point about the concept of language as a reflection of the culture is the fact that in Turkish culture there is a sharp dichotomy between males and females in all walks of village life, but there is almost no sex gender differentiation in the language. For example, there is only one third person singular pronoun, *O* which stands for he, she, or it, and the one feminine inflectional affix (-*e*, *müdür*, director; *müdüre*, female director) in the language is borrowed from Persian. Thus there seems to be a clear disharmony at this point between the culture and the language, unless one considers that the women are too insignificant to even be noticed.

To state that gramatical categories determine one's world view seems to be overstating the relationship. Certainly there is a high correlation between what appear to be natural categories in the language and culturally significant classes of reality. Whether this is a causal relationship either way or not, I am in no position to say. However, since both languages and cultures change almost constantly, and not necessarily at the same rate or in the same direction, it would seem that there will always be some incongruences.

Naturally the above description of Turkish structure is inadequate, but it is not possible to fully describe the grammar of any language in such a limited space. However, let us take one final example of the relationship between language and culture before going on to other things. So far we have been concerned only with the grammatical structure as if it were a lens through which Turks viewed the world. The frequency of usage of grammatical and lexical elements is another way of approaching this problem. For example, the passive voice in Turkish indicates that the subject of the verb is also the object of the action, for example, *yıkandı*, it was washed, rather than *yıkadı*, he washed it. This verb form is utilized very often by village Turks in conversation. This may indicate that they feel themselves buffeted by the world, Kismet, against which they are more or less helpless. This fact does not mean that they are passive in a psychological sense, only that they feel that resisting is more or less futile. This appears to me to coincide with their basic Islamic philosophy.

16

The Social Structure

DEMIRCILER is an endogamous village. This is unusual for Turkish villages, but Anatolia has been conquered by many different ethnic groups over the past 5000 years, and therefore villages retain different customs from past cultures. If a man from Demirciler married outside the village, he was forced by social pressures to leave the village. My informant knew of only two such cases in the history of the village.

According to folk history, three brothers, at some time in the distant past (perhaps 300 years ago, one informant said), had been forced to leave their ancestral home (no one seemed to have any idea of where this might have been). They separated, and one of the brothers founded Demirciler. Presumably one of the other brothers founded another village called Arap Köy, and I was told that it would be permissible for a young man or woman from Demirciler to marry someone from Arap Köy, since the people from that village would also be relatives.

The only principle that regulated marriage was a fear of marriage between "close" relatives. "Close" in this context means someone less than seven steps away. I asked repeatedly if one had to marry some special person in the village and was assured each time that this was not the case. To illustrate the system of steps, it is necessary to note that each house held an extended family which consisted of a man, his sons and wives and children, the sons' sons and wives and children, and so on. This household broke up either after the old man died or when he was very old. Thus each of the approximately 50 households contained from three to five generations of relatives. Now to the system of steps. Ego's parents were one step away from ego (ego being any individual), his parents' parents were two steps away, their parents were three steps away, so that anyone who did not live in ego's household, except those living in the household from which his mother came, was automatically three or four steps away from him. Now take a third household, any home in the village except the one from which his mother came and assume that the head of that household was a sibling of the head of his household. If the head of his household were his great grandfather (a fairly normal situation since marriage frequently took place at about 16 or 17 years of age and children usually arrived annually in the first few years of married life), he would be three steps away from ego. The head of the other household would be four steps from ego (if the two heads of households were siblings and farther if they were not), his children five, his grandchildren six, and his great grandchildren seven. Thus some of the children in any household in the village who were of ego's generation, except in that of ego's mother and his own, would be the proper distance from him. For a second example, assume that the head of a particular household was ego's great grandfather's first cousin. That would make the two heads of households three steps apart. Ego's great grandfather would be three steps away from ego. This would make ego six steps away from the head of the other household, seven steps away from his children, and eight steps away from anyone in ego's own generation in that household. Tracing the relationships through ego's mother, he would be two steps away from her parents (who would live in the household from which she came), three steps from her grandparents, one of whom would be in a third household, so that going in any direction, through either relative, ego could be no closer than three steps away from anyone in any household other than his own and that of his mother's father. This system prevented ego from marrying into either the extended family of his mother or father, but permitted his marriage with almost anyone else in the village in his generation.

Any village as small as Demirciler that practices endogamy over a long period of time will of necessity generate kinship ties among all of the members of the community, and there is little need in such a small group for any social organization other than that inherent in the kinship relationships. Status is acquired primarily by growing older. One old man, who seemed to be considered to be a dolt by everyone, was accorded the same formal respect as the village Muhtar, but it was given grudgingly and he obviously had less real status. However, he had much more status than any of the younger men, despite his ineptness in almost everything that the villagers considered to be important. As an indication of his position in the community, he was allowed to call prayers at times and always sat with the old men at the village meetings.

All men over 50 years of age ordered everyone else around, except men of their age or older, and I never saw anyone refuse to follow the orders. Old women ordered all of the other women around, but usually restricted their ordering of men to those quite young. All of the middle-aged men and women were able to order the young adults around, and so on down the line. As a matter of fact, anyone could give orders to anyone younger than himself of the same sex, but men could order women around who were older than they were.

Since status is partially determined by kinship, it is appropriate at this point to discuss briefly the system for labeling relatives in the village. In general, people are called by kinship terms, when addressed, rather than by name, especially if the individual addressed is older than the speaker. These terms of relationship reflect culturally significant groups of people much more than biological relationships. Kinship terminology is a system whereby the society groups the members of the community into classes for cultural reasons and has little to do with biological relationships. As a matter of fact few people outside the scientific world understand what biological relationship really means, the percentage of genes shared by ego (any given individual) and any given relative, and the particular gene pool from which these genes come. For example, ego and his mother share 50 percent of a certain group of genes, and ego and his father share 50 percent of a different pool of genes. Ego shares 25 percent of a certain gene pool with aunts and uncles on his father's side of the family and 25 percent of a different gene pool with aunts and uncles on his mother's side of the family, and so on. To relate this to the American system, the men and women we call aunts and uncles are related to us to the same degree, but those related through our father are not related in the same way, that is, do not share the same gene pool as those related through our mother, yet we use the same labels for both. The Turkish system makes this difference explicit, but obscures others—they have no terms for the people we would label cousins.

A few years ago some kinship systems were said to be classificatory and others were said to be descriptive. It can safely be said at this point that all kinship systems are classificatory and reflect a system of categories that is important to that culture and has only a secondary connection with biological relationships. To exemplify this with the system in use in Demirciler, consider the following classification in light of what has been said above. The de facto system, which differs somewhat from the theoretical one given by the informants, classifies the village population into three horizontal layers. All of the men and women two generations above ego were called terms meaning grandfather and grandmother. All men and women one generation older than ego were called by labels for aunts and uncles, except for one's own parents and siblings, and all villagers one generation younger than ego were called child.

The above described system that was observed to be operative in the village extends relationship terms to all of the villagers on the basis of relative age, whereas according to the system elicited from the informants, many of these people should not be called by kinship terms at all, though all knew that they were related and knew the lineage through which this relationship had been effected. According to the elicited system, father's and mother's mothers and their sisters were labeled *ebe* or *büyük anne* (alternately). Father's and mother's fathers and their brothers were labeled *dede* or *büyük baba*. One's biological mother was called *ana* (anne) and one's biological father was called *baba*. Mother's brother was called *dayı* and mother's sisters were called *teyze*. Father's brothers were called *amca*, and father's sisters were called *hala*. Older brothers were called *ağabey* and older sisters were called *abla*. Younger siblings were called *kardeş* regardless of sex. Thus older siblings were differentiated on the basis of sex, but younger ones were not. The children of mother's brothers were called *yiğin* (yeğen in standard Turkish) as were one's own sister's children. No other kinship terms could be elicited. Children of parent's brothers and sisters, people we would call cousins, are simply called by their name or described as *amcanın kızı* (literally father's brother's girl). The children of ego's brother were called *çocuk,* the same as one's own, and his children and his children's children were called *torun*, grandchild (regardless of sex), and children of grandchildren were also called *torun*.

One can grasp something of the significance of the kinship classification for the villagers by examining the meaning components of the kinship terms. Any person in the village who satisfies the criteria listed under "Meaning Components" is considered to be related to ego in the same manner, regardless of actual biological relationship.

TERMS	MEANING COMPONENTS
Büyük baba or *dede*	*Grandfather* Male Two generations older than ego In mother's or father's lineage
Büyük anne or *ebe*	*Grandmother* Female Two generations older than ego In mother's or father's lineage
Baba	*Father* Male Parent
Ana (*anne*)	*Mother* Female Parent
Amca	*Uncle* Male Parent's sibling Father's lineage
Hala	*Aunt* Female Parent's sibling Father's lineage
Dayı	*Uncle* Male Parent's sibling Mother's lineage
Teyze	*Aunt* Female Parent's sibling Mother's lineage
Yiğin (*yeğen*)	*Nephew and Niece* Child of *dayı, abla,* or female *kardeş*
Ağabey	*Elder brother* Male Sibling

	Older than ego
Abla	*Elder sister*
	Female
	Sibling
	Older than ego
Kardeş	*Younger brother and sister*
	Sibling
	Younger than ego
Çocuk	*Child*
	Child of ego or male
	kardeş
Torun	*Grandchild*
	Child of *çocuk*

Certain facts strike one almost immediately when looking at the meaning components listed above. Men and women are labeled differently for relatives older than ego, but not for those younger. Grandparents in both lineages are sharply differentiated on the basis of sex. In ego's generation children of ego's father's siblings have no labels nor do the children of mother's sister have any labels, but those of mother's brother are labeled the same as ego's own sister's children. Ego's older brothers and sisters have separate terms, but his younger brothers and sisters are lumped together with those of his brothers but distinguished from those of his sisters. Children of his sister's children are called only by name, but offspring of his children or those of his brothers are called grandchildren.

The kinship terms illustrate very well the sharp distinction between males and females in this culture as well as the sharp stratification into generational levels. People older than ego deserve his respect, but men must be respected much more than women, whereas everyone younger than ego must show respect for him. In terms of day to day activities, the men are nearly always working or talking in groups together in one place and the women in another. The young boys form a connecting link between these two socially isolated groups. As an example, the women cook the meals by themselves, and young boys bring the food to the table of the men. After the men have finished eating, the women and young boys eat what is left over.

Every house in the village has two separate living rooms, one for the men and one for the women, which serves to further separate the two sexes. Whenever the villagers are relaxing, the men are in the men's room and the women are in the women's room. Women come into the men's room rarely, usually to clean it when the men are away in the fields or when only the immediate family is present.

It is interesting to westerners to see this system in action. One day the "old Muhtar" (a man who had been the Muhtar for years but who had been voted out in the last election in favor of his younger brother, quite a revolutionary step for this village) asked us to come out to his home in the country (this house was about five miles from the village), and "have a drink of good, cool water or something."

The country houses are different from the town houses in that they are more crudely made. When we arrived at the house, we were met by the men en masse. They greeted us, and the old Muhtar's wife immediately took my wife aside and began to tell her about how much land her husband owned and so on, while the men were showing me the fields and groves. All of the young people (below the age of about 35) paid their respects by kissing the back of our hands, touching the spot kissed to their foreheads, and saying, *"hoş geldiniz"* (which means "come with pleasantness," their way of saying welcome).

A virtual army of women and young boys (teenagers) were busy preparing something for us in a shady spot about 150 yards from the house. Just past noon we were led down to this spot, which was on the edge of a stream of water about two feet wide and a foot deep that bubbled up out of the ground only about ten feet away. Here we found that heavy reed mats had been spread over the ground with beautiful, hand-woven carpets on top of them, to cover an area about fifteen feet square, and a large number of small pillows lay here and there on the carpets. I was immediately given the seat of honor (as a guest anyone would have been so honored) at the corner of the carpeting nearest the spring. The other men sat or half-reclined on either side with the older men nearest me, and the younger ones farther away. The women and boys carried large trays and pots of food down from the house as we talked about the weather, crops, and so on. After a time one of the boys brought a circular wooden stand about ten inches high, and another boy placed on it a large copper tray containing a whole roasted lamb, curled around in a circle so that it just filled the tray. The host began to cut pieces off the lamb and handed one to me first, then he distributed the meat to the other men in order of age. He also handed out large pieces of bread along with the meat. Incidentally, my wife was treated as a man in this particular situation and most of the time, for that matter, because the villagers really did not know what to do with foreign women. She was served after me, but before the men from the village.

When everyone had eaten his fill, one of the large number of women, on a hand signal from the host, pointed to the tray and looked at a young boy who seemed to be hovering about waiting for orders. He immediately removed the tray and put a large pot of rice in its place. After we had had our fill of this, several other courses were brought, eaten, and taken away, and the meal was terminated with a tray of grapes, on which we munched as we talked until suddenly, without warning, it began to rain and everyone grabbed something and headed for the house. By the time we reached the house however, it had stopped raining. Since the party had been more or less broken up by the change in weather, we thanked our hosts and headed back for the village.

Going back now to the sharp separation between men and women, the women ate nothing at all until the men were completely finished and had their tray of grapes to occupy them for a time. Then one of the boys made Turkish coffee. This is made by placing finely powdered coffee and sugar in a cup and pouring boiling water over this mixture. This sets for a few minutes and is drunk, coffee grounds and all. The boy served coffee to me first, then my wife, and finally to all the other men in order of age, beginning with the oldest. During this part of the meal the women were eating by themselves on the ground, some distance away, as we (the men) rested comfortably on the carpets and talked. This veritable feast was the "cool drink of water or something" that the host had referred to in his invitation the day before.

The episode above will serve as an illustration of two very important mechanisms that control social interaction within the village, the male versus female dichotomy, and age. The old men, and guests (hospitality is of extreme importance to these people as it is with nearly all of the peoples in the Middle East) always sit in a place of honor and are served, guests first in order of age, then the old men in order of age, beginning with the oldest and working down to the youngest. At indoor gatherings of the men, the old people sit on a raised, couchlike projection, which is built out from the wall, and the rest of the men and boys sit on the floor. At the same time the women gather in another room and prepare food and tea for the men. The older women when present receive respectful treatment similar to that of the men. The young boys bring the food into the men's room. The above illustrates the most important way in which interpersonal relationships within the village operate.

Thus we have a society broken up into effective social classes, but these all involve basically (1) sex and (2) age, as opposed to money, position, or title. The society could be visualized as forming a "Y" with all children at the bottom, regardless of sex. The circumcised boys are somewhat above girls and uncircumcised boys. Married men and women form two separate groups, both of which outrank (and hence can give orders to) the children. The class of young married women outranks only the children, and the young married men outrank young married women and children. Within each class, if you are older than someone else, you outrank him. The two classes of old married men and old married women outrank everyone in some way, but the old women do not often try to give orders to any men except the unmarried ones, that is, members of the class labeled children.

Probably the most unhappy members of the community are newly married girls. These young women are called *gelin,* which when translated into English, means literally the word "come" and one hears constantly the sound of this word about the village as everyone in the family, except the children, call *gelin* do this, *gelin* do that. The girl must uphold the dignity of her family by proving to her husband's family that she can take all of this without whimpering and do everything that they ask well. Throughout Turkey a high percentage of mental breakdowns are said to occur among young married women. The period of adjustment immediately following marriage begins the day after the wedding and usually lasts for about three years (sometimes as long as five) in Demirciler, though it may differ in different villages. The period can be less if a younger brother gets married and brings a new *gelin* into the household and longer if not, unless the husband can persuade the family to voluntarily release the girl, which he may do if he loves her very much and feels sorry for her. If the family agrees to this, then the man gives his wife a gift and tells her that she is now *hanım* (wife), not *gelin* (bride).

Achieved status occurs within the community, but generally speaking one always outranks those in the younger age groups, and has relatively high versus low status only with respect to other members of his own generation, that is, other old men or other young men. Problems are already developing in this area of the social order, however. One of the manifestations of this class organization is the use of terms for aunts and uncles for everyone in your father's age group (assuming that you are an unmarried male *or* female), the use of grandparent terms for men and women in your grandfather's age group, and proper names for your age-mates or occasionally the kinship terms for older brother or older sister, and children for members of your children's generation. Under the old system all boys were married before going into the military service. As a result they entered the young married group at approximately 19 years of age, but my principal informant was still unmarried at 22. He called all of the old men "uncle," because they belonged to his father's generation, even though he was technically a member of the class of unmarried boys. Partially because of his education, I believe, as well as his age, he was always with the young married people rather than the unmarried ones. His was the only such case to my knowledge in 1961, but this will be an increasing problem as the young people who are in school now go on to higher education and fail to marry at the traditional age.

Since all of the villagers were farmers, there appeared to be no special interest groups such as craft guilds, except the extended families, each of which was principally interested in its own improvement. This was not a significant thing in this particular village, however, as everyone considered himself a member of a single larger family unit, and thus bound to promote the welfare of the village as a whole.

While the social organization controlled most of the activities in the village, political power had long been recognized, but generally as something external. In the days of the Ottoman (*Osmanlı*) Empire, the power of the central government was felt only when taxes were not paid or some gesture of disrespect (such as refusal to go into the army at the proper time) was made toward the Sultan. Because of the absolute power of the Sultanate, villagers were usually careful not to offend the government. This natural cautiousness and the remoteness of Istanbul made intervention from the outside rare. The link between the village and this remote central government had always been the Muhtar, the oldest male in Demirciler, as he was the head of the kinship group.

The above situation has changed considerably in recent years and is likely to change still more in the years to come. Under the Republic it is required by law that the Muhtar be an elective office. From 1923 until the mid-fifties this had little effect, as the villagers simply voted the oldest man back into office at each election. However, in the last election held under the Menderes government the old Muhtar was voted out of office in favor of the next oldest man in the village. It seems likely that as the very large crop of young people go through the public schools, learn more about democratic processes, and mature to become voters, still younger men will be elected to this office until finally it will become truly elective.

The national political organization in Turkey is a constitutional republic. Since the revolution in 1960 a new constitution has been approved with a two house Parliament, instead of the single house established under Ataturk. The new constitution embodies many checks and balances not incorporated in the old system, and the country now has four major political parties instead of the two established by Atatürk. So far as the village was concerned, however, in 1960 there was only one party, the Democrats. Since this party has been outlawed, I do not know what has replaced it.

The country is divided into *vilayets,* roughly translated as provinces, which are about the size of counties in the American Middle West. Each of these provinces has a fairly large city as its capital, and the province has the same name as the city. Demirciler is a part of the Vilayet of Kaman.

Within the *vilayet* each town, consisting of a population of between 3000 and 8000, has a certain area around it that is called a *kaza,* which could be compared with American counties but are much smaller. Demirciler is also in the Kaza of Kaman.

Under the Republic the village has three elective officers: the village Bekçi (watchman), the field Bekçi, and the Muhtar. All of these men draw cash salaries from the central government.

Within the village there are no other political groups. There is no village council of any kind, except the winter meetings of all the men in the Muhtar's house. All males are allowed to come to these meetings, and all adult males participate in the discussions. This group debates and decides on all issues concerning the village in a very democratic manner, except that the women are excluded. So far the village has been small enough for this type of "town meeting" to work quite well. However, it will be interesting to see the changes that take place in the years to come as the population increases and many of the young people grow up and take up trades and occupations other than farming. This will undoubtedly produce more different factions as each occupational group begins to fight for its own best interest. This factor has not been encountered in this completely agricultural society up to now.

17

Islam, a Way of Life

THE RELIGION of Mahmud's village is Islam, called the Mohammedan religion by many westerners, and occasionally the Moslem or Muslim religion. Allah is believed to be the only true God, and He is the same God worshipped by all of the believers in the Book, Jews, Christians, and Moslems, all of whom are on the right road, in contrast with pagans who are doomed because they do not recognize the true God.

Only the followers of Mohammed are doing exactly what Allah wants men to do, however. Basically, the village Turk believes that the Jews started off properly, but slipped off the right path occasionally. God was forced to send Prophets to correct their ways, and then after awhile they would err again and another Prophet would have to be sent. Christ came to lead the people back into the fold, but Christians made the horrible mistake of forgetting God and worshipping Christ. Then Mohammed came along to put the world on the right path. The true "believers" of Islam object to being called Mohammedans because this implies worship of Mohammed, and he was only a Prophet. One old man went to great lengths one day to explain to me that Christ did not die on the cross as Christians believe. Allah removed him and placed a man "who looked like Christ" in his place.

One of the basic values incorporated in the religion of Islam is that of submission to the will of God. One seeks to become a part of God's great plan for mankind and the world by making it possible for Him to use one as an instrument for His work. The belief in this overriding plan is constantly referred to with the word *inşallah* that follows the statement of any proposed project or intended future action. *Inşallah* is usually translated as "I hope," "I hope so," or "if God wills it." I believe that a better translation would be "if this fits in with God's plans," as it seems to me that this is the thought that the village "believers" are trying to express.

The Moslem religion is based on a combination of Biblical teachings and the Arabic culture extant in the vicinity of Mecca during the seventh

86

century A.D. as blended and modified by Mohammed (570–632) A.D.). The Prophet, as Mohammed is called, was born into a family of religious leaders in Mecca, but was orphaned at an early age. After the death of his parents he lived for awhile with his grandparents, but was again orphaned while still very young. His uncle, a caravaneer, raised the boy and took him on many long trips with his caravans. On these trips Mohammed learned a great deal about the values of Arabic culture and how to be a successful man in that society. He must have learned these lessons well since he became very successful in nearly all walks of Arabic life. When he was twenty-five he married a widow and managed her money so well that they became quite wealthy. He was in his forties when he began to have visions. At first he felt that he might be losing his mind, but was finally convinced that Allah had chosen him to be His messenger and sent the Angels with His word.

Mohammed is not thought of by the Turkish villagers, or Moslems in general for that matter, as being different from mortal men, except that God chose him for a special task. His birth was normal as was his death. Many of his followers are said to have been disturbed immediately after his death by the fact that he had just died as any other man. However, the chosen few finally remembered many things Mohammed had told them, and interpreted these in such a way that they were sure he had predicted he would die just as anyone else and that they were not to revere or worship him as a Diety. Mohammed, in contrast with Christ, lived a long life and was a success as a businessman and a military leader in addition to his religious teachings. As a matter of fact, much of the success of Islam was probably due to Mohammed's genius as a military leader. His achievements were attributed to the fact that God was leading him, and the people believed this. Further, the teachings of Mohammed fitted naturally in with the culture of the Arabs at that time. In contrast, Christ was attempting to replace many of the values of his culture with new, and what he considered to be, better and more universal values. The two factors given above were among the most important ones that accounted for the rapid spread of Islam throughout all of the Middle East.

The villagers do not make a distinction, common to Americans and Europeans in general, between the religious and the secular. Islam is a way of life and is the dominant factor in the making of any decision, no matter how slight, in the mind of a villager. The Koran (the equivalent of the Bible in Islam) and associated writings (these include a great many things that were reportedly said by Mohammed at various times during his life), are always consulted when one is in doubt as to what course of action is the proper one.

The religion is basically fatalistic in that no one can really go against the Will of Allah, but it is considerably more than that. The true Moslem not only resigns himself to the inevitable Will of God, but attempts to be of significant help in putting this plan into operation.

The five pillars of Islam are very important to the villagers. First, one must pray five times a day, at sunup, midmorning, at noon, midafternoon, and at sundown, confessing his belief in Allah as the one and only true God and Mohammed as His Prophet. This is done quite regularly by some of the villagers and not so regularly by most. The regularity increases near feast days and religious holidays. Second, one must give alms to the poor. What one gives need not be large or expensive, but one must give; it is the fact of giving that is important. Third, one must fast during the sacred month of Ramazan (Ramadan in Arabic). This fasting means not eating, drinking, smoking, or having contact with women from a specified time before sunrise to a specified time after sunset. The villagers arise very early during this period and eat a large meal before beginning the day's fast. Nothing is eaten after that, except by menstruating women or people who are ill, until after nightfall. During this period the evening meal is huge because everyone is starved by nightfall. Fourth, one must sacrifice a lamb on the Kurban Bayram and give a portion of the meat to the poor. Fifth, a good Moslem must make a pilgrimage to Mecca or have someone make it for him. I do not know of anyone in the village who had made the pilgrimage in 1961, but there might have been someone there. In any event, making the trip to Mecca is very difficult for the villagers. However, with their ever-increasing standard of living and better communications with the outside world, it may become within their reach, at least for some of the wealthier ones, in the near future.

The new mosque is the finest building in the village. It is made of natural stone and has a tile roof. It is a square building with small windows on all sides and is surrounded by a stone wall. The gate in the wall and the door on the entrance are both handmade from raw wood and left unpainted, as are nearly all door and window frames in the village. The area within the wall is barren. Three young trees have been planted in recent years and are barely surviving with considerable care. Inside the building the walls are white and the floors are covered with carpets. In each of the two corners furthest from the door is a pulpitlike structure. The one on the right has a stairway leading to a square platform without a canopy. The latter is considerably larger than the other platform (which is the traditional type found in all the other mosques I visited) and is draped with a brilliant red goat-hair rug. This platform is used on holy days whereas the more traditional one is used on ordinary Fridays. Services are held every Friday at the time of the midday prayer and also on feast days. The service consists of a formal prayer followed by an address by the Hoca wherein he admonishes the villagers to follow the path of the true believer.

The Hoca is one of the few persons in the village who draws a cash salary from the central government; one of Menderes' reforms put into effect in the late 1950s. This is in sharp contrast with the system of separation of the state from the church established by Ataturk. The Hoca is responsible for the spiritual life of the village as well as the management of the mosque and its properties. Once a year there is a collection from all of the villagers for the mosque. The Hoca will bring up this matter one evening as the men sit around talking in the Muhtar's house, and with all, or nearly all, of the men present, the group will discuss the amount needed. The discussion continues until there is complete agreement. Then the group gets down to who is going to pay how much. The Muhtar may suggest that a certain man should give so much. The

Hoca may agree or suggest more or less, usually the man will say that whatever amount he is asked to give is too much. Then much debate ensues, finally ending when a figure, satisfactory to all concerned, is reached. At a later time the Muhtar and Hoca jointly collect this levy. When asked about the possibility that someone might not pay the levy, the villagers said that this could not happen. Probably it never has, but it seems likely to this writer that as urbanization of the village progresses, the possibility of such a refusal also increases until someone in the not too distant future is likely to refuse to pay. This will pose a serious stress situation, for there is no apparent mechanism for handling such a refusal other than public rebuke, which currently is sufficient but may not be in the future.

In addition to the formal religion, all Turkish villages have many folk-beliefs. I do not have detailed data for Demirciler on this subject, but belief in the evil-eye is common, and the villagers in Demirciler displayed the ever-present blue beads that are thought to be a protection against this menace. A well-known physician (an eye specialist, incidentally) in Ankara told me quite seriously one day that the evil-eye was not a supernatural phenomenon at all. He theorized that certain wave lengths in light were harmful to human beings and that certain people had the ability to store up these harmful wave lengths and release them at will. These frequencies when directed toward an individual (children were supposed to be most susceptible to these), cause poor health and can result in a general deterioration ending in death. He did not explain how the blue beads served to protect one from this.

Another example of folk-beliefs, which occurred in Ankara, but is similar to those found throughout Anatolia, concerns love portents. One day our neighbor's wife came out of her house screaming hysterically. My wife and another neighbor brought her into our house and calmed her down. Then she explained that her husband had a mistress in an apartment on the other side of town. The wife had felt oil on the door frame in her front hallway and she believed that if another woman puts fish oil around a door and a man walks through it, he will have to love her. The fear of losing her husband had caused the hysterical outburst. However, when we left Ankara over a year later her husband was still living at home.

One final example, a doctor in Ankara asked me to drive him to Istanbul one day because he had no driver's license—for he was a menace behind the wheel and this the Turkish police were aware of. As we started the engine he said, "Maşallah." I asked why he said that and was informed that if one said "Maşallah" when he started the engine, a safe journey was guaranteed.

The folk-beliefs described above are typical of those in Demirciler and throughout Anatolia. These are not a part of Islam any more than superstitions are a part of Christianity, but exist along with the religion as something separate from it. There appears to be no conflict between these beliefs and the Moslem doctrine, however.

18

Education

THE MORES and activities of the village are transmitted by example rather than in a formal teaching situation. Children have no schedule and are rarely punished. Very young children awaken early in the morning, are given some bread and fruit, grapes or black olives, and out they go. Very young boys play, listen to the men talk, or watch their elders as they work, and the girls stay close to their mothers. Both sexes seem anxious to learn the tasks of their parents and are permitted to do so as soon as the older ones feel that they are capable. During six and one-half years residence in Turkey, I saw only one parent strike a child and this was considered to be a terrible thing. As the children repeat a job and become succesful at it, this work becomes more or less permanent. Most of the disciplining observed was in the form of mild scolding and was administered by an older brother or sister as a rule, not a parent.

As an example of the haphazard way in which the children were brought up, we were always amused by the procedure, or more accurately the lack of any procedure, at bedtime. In the evening the children played outside until they decided to come in. Once inside they were petted, loved, and allowed to go about their business until they fell asleep somewhere about the house. They were allowed to remain wherever they were until it was convenient for some adult to put them to bed, which was done without awakening the child in so far as this was possible.

Until recently there was only one formal situation in which the children learned and that was the mosque school. There the children memorized parts of the Koran in Arabic. Each day the Hoca would sit in the mosque and recite from the Koran in Arabic, and the children would attempt to repeat exactly what he said without understanding it at all. The villagers believe that a prayer or part of the Koran must be repeated perfectly, and only in Arabic, to be effective.

Now there is the school near Kaman to which the great majority of children go each day. All of the boys have been going to school since about 1950, and well-qualified graduates can go on to middle school (junior high school), as it is called, and then on to *lise* (high school) after that. Not all towns the size of Kaman have *lises,* but there are a limited number of government scholarships so that the better students can go to boarding schools in other towns when high schools are not available. Very few villagers had even finished the grade school of Kaman in 1961, but nearly all of the young ones of today will finish. This, I am sure, will release great revolutionary influences in the years to come as formal school education will of necessity conflict with the traditional way of life of the villagers. The school curriculum is controlled from Ankara by the Ministry of Education, which has as one of its avowed purposes the modernization of the country, especially the villages. In 1961 the villagers were still pretty much a homogeneous lot with the same system of values, but the school is now instilling new values in the young. Conflict is inevitable in such a situation, and some of the children are likely to look on the way of life of their families as degrading, whereas in the past they have looked to their families for guidance in what was good or bad.

The most important semiformal situation for learning so far as the boys are concerned are the evening meetings at the home of the Muhtar. During the cold months of winter, there is little to do in the evening and fuel is scarce. Presumably because of this shortage of fuel, the men all gathered in the men's room of the Muhtar's house just about dark almost every evening.

In the late afternoon the women of the Muhtar's family clean up the room, put wood in the fireplace, and place dishes of fruit here and there. Then shortly after the evening meal each man comes, as suits his fancy. The Muhtar seats himself in the center of the benchlike projection. This is not sat on as we would use a chair, but the men fold their legs up beneath them as one might sit on the ground. This seating area is for prestige, not comfort. Only the very old men are permitted to sit there.

The men on the right and left of the Muhtar are the oldest men in the village. The seating is arranged so that about twelve of the oldest men are seated on both sides of the Muhtar in order of descending age. However, I am not sure that it is actually that carefully worked out, but at least the older men do sit in the middle and the younger of the old men sit toward the end. The young men and boys spread themselves out on the floor as they please. No women are allowed in this room at all and young boys are permitted to stay only so long as they sit quietly. If a child does anything to disturb the men in their debates, an older boy, 10 to 13 years of age, will remove him as quickly and quietly as possible.

It is at these evening meetings at the Muhtar's house that a boy learns the values of village culture and how to fulfill his role as a man in the society. Until very recently these meetings were attended by all males in the community. With the expanding population this may not even now be possible because all the males cannot crowd into one room. When this mechanism ceases to function, as it must soon, the centuries old chain of cultural transmission will be broken. It was here that a boy learned the place of women, the way he should treat his elders, and much of the technology in the village. He was not taught these things specifically, but absorbed information and ideas through a kind of intellectual osmosis as the older men discussed their problems and the problems in the village.

The evening begins with idle conversation among friends. This is completely spontaneous and continues until nearly everyone has arrived. Then several different things could happen. Someone could address a question to the Muhtar, such as what should be done about someone's teen-aged son who was watching the girls too much. If so, this problem is generally hashed about, frequently with the boy present, and finally a suitable punishment arrived at. The boy's father or elder brother is then responsible for carrying out the punishment. The discussion of the case publicly is usually sufficient to make the offender mend his ways without any overt punishment, unless the person is a repeater. The young learn by hearing the discussion just what is expected of them as they grow up.

Other topics taken up at these meetings include such things as when the taxes are due, the annual levy for the mosque, the building of a new road, wall, or bridge in or near the village, and so on. Work projects are usually done by the young men, without pay, and the Muhtar picks the crew and tells them what to do. A young man's prestige will depend to a large extent on how well he does these jobs and in general how well he follows the norms of the community. Since all of the men meet together frequently and discuss all problems until a unanimous decision is reached, there are fairly sharply defined rules of conduct that all follow. For example, one must always defer to an older person when he speaks, one must not strike his parents, and so on. If someone does something serious, such as strike his father, the Muhtar and village Bekçi could call the Jandarma and haul the boy into court in Kaman, but this is almost never necessary. I did not observe any breaches of conduct while in the village. In general everyone seemed to follow the rules quite closely, but perhaps my presence influenced their behavior somewhat, I do not know. The kinds of possible misconduct were indicated by my informants when I asked about them.

It is difficult for a man to get accurate information on women in a Moslem society because of the sharp segregation of the sexes. There may be a semiformal situation wherein women learn about their roles too, but I am not aware of anything comparable with the men's daily meetings. The women are usually in their own homes doing housework while the men are discussing village business at the home of the Muhtar. Their daughters are with the women in the home and learn their womanly roles from their mothers and other female kin.

19

Folklore and Superstition

CLASSIFICATION of folklore is always difficult, but the stories from Demirciler fall into at least three genre: (1) *Hoca* stories, (2) *Keloğlan* stories, and (3) others. The latter category is the ever-present scientific wastebasket and probably includes several distinct classes of tales. Types (1) and (2) are distinctive in being culture hero tales, but with different heroes and having an entirely different quality. The hero for type (1) is Nesreddin Hoca (a religious teacher). These stories are very realistic in the sense that nothing supernatural occurs in them. The Hoca is sometimes wise and sometimes foolish, but there is always something humorous about the tale. These stories are usually very short and are found by the hundreds all over Turkey. While traveling, passing an afternoon, or at a party, men will get to telling "hoca stories" and each one leads to another one. The hero for type (2) is a youth called Keloğlan. It seems, according to some informants, that there was once a boy who liked fairy tales so much that he gradually shut himself away from reality until at last he found himself living in a fairylike world. In the Keloğlan tales nearly everything is supernatural. In type (3) there are stories about villagers and many animal stories wherein animals are given human characteristics. These stories usually teach the village child something about how he should live, or exalt masculine intelligence as opposed to feminine ignorance, and one that I collected was an explanation for the formation of a group of peculiarly shaped rocks near Kaman.

Most Turkish folktales begin with *Bir varmış, bir yokmuş,* which translates very roughly *one there was one there wasn't,* but is equivalent to *once upon a time. Bir varmış bir yokmuş, bir Hoca varmış.* Once upon a time there was a Hoca. His name was Nesreddin Hoca, and one day a priest invited him to dinner. The priest had a wonderful meal with many good things to eat, but when the Hoca was offered some ham, he refused it saying that his religion would not allow him to eat pork. The priest understood, but remarked, "what joys you have missed."

At a later date the Hoca invited the priest to his home for dinner, and the Hoca's wife fixed a delicious meal. As they were eating, the Hoca's wife brought them food, and finally the Hoca asked the priest why he had never married. The priest replied that his religion would not allow him to do so. To this the Hoca responded with, "what joys you have missed," with a twinkle in his eye.

Keloğlan is quite a different kind of character, and it is simpler to illustrate with a story than to try to explain. *Bir varmış bir yokmuş evvel zaman içinde,* once upon a time in the days of long ago when bears were barbers, camels were middlemen, and when I was rocking my father's cradle, my father fell out of it, and my mother fell down too. One of them took a switch and the other took a pair of tongs, and I ran away. After traveling a great distance, I came to a town where I saw an old woman with many children sitting around her listening to a tale. I sat down with them and listened too.

Many years ago a man had three sons. They had a wheatfield, and shortly after the three boys reached manhood someone started stealing their wheat. The father sent his eldest son to guard the field, but the young man fell asleep, and when he woke up, he saw that the wheat was all gone. The next year the father sent his second son to watch the field, but he too went to sleep, the same as his older brother had, and when he woke up, all of the wheat was gone again. A year later the youngest and most intelligent son was sent to the field. The name of this son was Keloğlan (the boy with no hair). The youngest boy climbed into a tree and waited. At midnight three horses appeared suddenly and began to eat the wheat. Keloğlan jumped to the ground and caught the three horses.

The animals pleaded with Keloğlan, "please let us go. Take three hairs from each of us. When you burn these hairs we will come to help you."

Keloğlan did what they said and let them go. Time passed and the father died, and all of the boys set up homes of their own. One day the Sultan of the town announced that his daughter would be married to the winner of the horse contest. Everyone in the town went to watch the contest, and the brothers of Keloğlan went too, but did not take him with them. After they had gone Keloğlan burned the hairs from one of the horses that he had caught in his father's fields. In an instant a black horse and a black suit of clothes appeared. Keloğlan put on the suit and went to the place where the contest was to be held. The contest was to see if any one of the contestants could break a very heavy chain that the Sultan had made for the occasion. All of the horses from the city tried to break the chain, but all failed. Keloğlan with his black horse did, however, break the chain easily. Then he took the girl and a bag of gold and went to his home before his brothers. When they came he asked them what had happened at the contest. They told him that a man dressed in black and riding a black horse had broken the chain and taken the Sultan's daughter away. Nobody suspected Keloğlan.

Some days later the Sultan announced that he would marry his second daughter. (Turks always marry daughters in order of age with the eldest being married first) to the winner of another contest. Again the older brothers went and left Keloğlan at home. Again he burned one of the hairs taken from the horses he had captured in his father's fields. This time a white horse appeared along with a white suit of clothes. Keloğlan put on the white suit and rode to the place where the contest was to be held. The Sultan had a large hole filled with water, and the contest was to see if any of the horses could jump over this hole. All of the horses fell in the water, but Keloğlan and his white horse made it easily, and he took the girl and a bag of gold home with him when he went. When the sisters saw each other they were very surprised.

Then the Sultan wanted to marry his third daughter who was the most beautiful of all with the youth who could win another contest. The brothers went as before, leaving Keloğlan at home. He burned one of the hairs as before, and the third horse, a red one, appeared with a red suit of clothes. Keloğlan put on the red suit and rode off to the contest. This time there was to be a race, and the girl was to be married to the man with the quickest horse. Of course Keloğlan won the race and took the girl to his house with some gold. When the sisters saw each other they were very surprised.

The next night Keloğlan invited his brothers to dinner. At first they didn't want to go to his house, but when he said, "I have a surprise for you," they decided to go anyway. When they arrived at Keloğlan's stable, they were surprised to see the three horses inside. Then they went inside and saw the Sultan's three daughters. Then they were really surprised. Keloğlan gave the oldest girl and the black horse to his eldest brother, and the second girl and the white horse to the second brother. Then he said that he would marry the youngest one himself. The jealous brothers saw that he had kept the most beautiful girl and all of the gold for himself.

That night the brothers thought of ways of getting these things from Keloğlan. The next day they called Keloğlan and took him to a deep well far outside the town. The second brother had gone to the well earlier and thrown some gold into it. When they arrived at the well, the brothers told Keloğlan that there was a great deal of gold in the well and that they were going to tie a rope around him and lower him into the well so that he could get the gold. They began to let him down into the well, but when he was almost halfway to the bottom, the brothers cut the rope, and he fell the rest of the way. Then he understood that it was a trap and began to look around for a way out. He found a hole there at the bottom, and when he went through the hole, he came out into a country under the earth. He went to a small house, knocked on the door and an old woman came out. He asked her for a glass of water. When the water came, Keloğlan noticed that it had a very bad taste and smell.

"Why is the water so bad, and where am I?" Keloğlan asked the old woman.

The woman said that this was the country under the ground, and that there was only one fountain in the country. Once each year a giant came to the country to eat a young girl and after having eaten the girl he would open the fountain. This year there were no more girls left, so the Sultan's daughter was to be eaten. Keloğlan went to where the old lady had said that the fountain was, and there he saw the girl. She told him to go away because the giant would eat him also, but he didn't go. After a very short time, they heard the giant coming in the distance. When he saw two people instead of one, he became even more hungry and ran toward them. Keloğlan whipped out his sword and cut off the giant's head. At that time the girl made a mark on Keloğlan's back with the giant's blood.

After killing the giant Keloğlan went to the home of the old woman, and the girl went to the palace of her father. When the Sultan saw that his daughter was alive and that the fountain was open again, he was very happy. The Sultan decided to give his daughter in marriage to this brave young man. He announced to all the country that everyone would have to pass before him under a bridge in front of the palace. When Keloğlan passed under with the others, the girl knew him because of the mark on his back. The sultan wanted him to marry his daughter, but Keloğlan said that he was already married. Then the Sultan asked Keloğlan if he wanted anything at all from him, and Keloğlan answered that he would like a chance to think about it for awhile before stating his wish. Then he left the palace.

After going about the country for a while, Keloğlan lay down beneath a tree and went to sleep. Suddenly, he was awakened by the noise of a snake. When he opened his eyes, he saw a snake about to eat some baby birds. He killed the snake and went back to sleep again. Later the mother bird came and she was very, very big. At first she thought that Keloğlan was an enemy and wanted to kill him, but the babies stopped her. They told their mother that he had saved their lives from the snake, who was lying nearby, dead. When she saw the dead snake, the mother bird was very happy and spread her wings to make a shade so that Keloğlan could sleep better. Later, when he woke up, he was frightened at first, because the big bird was hovering over him. However, when the bird began to speak to him, his fears passed. The bird said, "What do you want from me?" Keloğlan answered that he wanted to go up above to earth to his own country. "All right," said the bird, "but I want 40 pieces of meat and 40 drinks of water. When I say, 'gak', you will have to give me some meat, and when I say, 'guk', you will have to give me some water as we travel up to the land above."

Keloğlan then went to the Sultan (of the Kingdom below the ground) and obtained the things that the bird wanted. Then they began their flight. During the trip, when the bird said "gak" he gave her meat, and when she said "guk" he gave her water. After a very long time they came to the surface of the earth. Keloğlan went directly to the palace of the Sultan (of the Turkish Empire) and told his story. The Sultan became very angry and called the bad brothers to him. When they arrived they were very surprised to see Keloğlan alive. They asked him to excuse them, saying that they were very sorry. Keloğlan forgave his brothers and gave a feast that lasted for 40 days and 40 nights, and finally married his beautiful girl and began to live in the Sultan's palace.

Genre number (3), labelled "others," contains animal stories, one of which involves a husband and wife snake with very human characteristics; some "how-so" stories, as well as love stories; and others about ordinary people. This grouping undoubtedly could be broken up into two or three distinctive types if more data were available. The story given in Chapter 4 about the foolish woman and her three daughters illustrates one kind of tale from genre (3). A short "how-so" story about a bride and her sheep being turned into stone, included in Chapter 7, illustrates the difference between these two types and, perhaps, should be set up as different genre. This was not done because there is no clear-cut structural feature (such as a particular culture hero with sharply defined attributes) that differentiates stories in genre (3) from each other.

Turkish folklore is very rich and in villages such as Demirciler still very much alive. The above examples certainly do not begin to show either the variety or richness of the folk tales. This would require a large volume in itself.

Folk songs have not been mentioned so far, but the people of Demirciler love to sing. Most of the songs are about unrequited love or dying, and by American standards are real tearjerkers. These songs do not use any of the traditional Western scales. A friend of mine was talking with a Turk about some note she had just heard and wanted to know if the note were F or F#. The Turk said that it was halfway between these two notes. This, my ethnocentric friend could not accept and said, "There isn't any note between F and F#." To this the Turk replied, "No?" Took up his ute, struck F, then F#, and moved his finger halfway between the position for F and F# and struck the strings of the instrument. The American said, "but that isn't a note," to which the Turk again replied, "what is it then?"

The point is that they use a scale that is made up of steps that do not coincide with the Western scale at all. Consequently, the music sounds harsh and unmelodic to westerners at first. However, I acquired a definite taste for this music and thoroughly enjoy listening to it even when I do not understand what is being sung, but this is a taste that has to be acquired by most westerners.

I will give the words from one of these songs so that the reader can see just how melancholy they really are.

> I am sick and cannot hold my pencil in my hand.
> I wonder if I can see my birthplace.
> Give my regards to my father.
> Look at my picture and cry.
> If my father asks, "where is my (name of the singer)."
> Don't tell him where I have gone.
> The world is like a gear turning backwards.
> Whoever is waiting for me will look down the road and cry.
> In the distance I see Çankira mountain.
> There is a big cemetery near the hospital.
> They will write (name of the singer) on the tombstone.

The sound of the music is almost like a long low wail, and one word will be held for ten to fifteen seconds as the music shifts from one note to another, and it is very difficult to understand the words as they are being sung even when they are very familiar to you.

The above translation completely obscures the rhyme scheme of the song, as an attempt was made only to translate the ideas involved, not the quality of the poetry.

20

Conclusion

Nothing has been said so far about the theory of how human groups are organized into structured wholes. The description given above has attempted to present as accurately and straightforwardly as possible an objective picture of the life in the village. What do we mean by an objective description? Let us consider briefly the real world, that is the physical universe in which we all as human beings find ourselves attempting to cope with the exigencies of everyday life. This universe is frequently referred to by scientists as infinite, both in the time dimension and the spacial dimension. Now, the problem of dealing with human beings is that the human mind does not seem to be capable of dealing effectively with infinite quantities, especially if these happen to be continuous rather than discreet. Thus, everywhere, where man is found, he classifies the things about him into groups or classes so that he can react to every member of a particular group as if these entities were all the same and thus handle the universe comfortably. The problem, in so far as cultural descriptions are concerned, arises from the fact that the Turkish villager does not categorize this universe in the same way that the anthropologist does. The latter is a product of another totally different kind of culture. It is extremely difficult and important for the scientist to describe the categories that are important to the villager, not the categories that are important to the anthropologist.

Kinship terms are easy to use as examples of the above described system of classification, though social classes and many other phenomena would serve equally well. Every individual has a group of people who are related to him in specific biological ways, that is, he shares certain percentages of his genes with certain other people as a result of his descent from a particular set of parents. Therefore, if cultures were much concerned with the reality involved in these relationships, one would find that kinship systems were much the same the world over, but this is not the case. Many people whom we call cousins are not normally thought of as relatives by Turks, and different biological relationships, mother's sister and father's sisters, are lumped together by Americans, when they are obviously not related to us in the same manner. The Turk on the other hand differentiates these relatives to show that one is related through the mother and the other through the father. Both are called aunts in English, but *hala* means father's sister and *teyze* means mother's sister.

The above example is a rather obvious one, and anthropologists have not been overly troubled by this type of classification in recent years, but beginning students often fail to realize the importance of such differential classification of the world about us. However, ethnologists in attempting to describe material culture have continued frequently to list an infinite number of specifics, giving a wide variety of detail without differentiating between the essential and the accidental. However, it is impossible to describe every physical variation found in any culture for any given element, be it material or nonmaterial in nature, so that any description represents some kind of classification. These classes should reflect the relationship that these elements have to each other within the cultural system. The problem is, how does one determine which elements should be classified together? Anthropology does not have a widely accepted methodology for determining the significance of elements as does, for example, the field of linguistics. Because of this lack of methodology, many field workers simply attempt to describe as much of the objective evidence as possible, knowing full well that they cannot give all of it, but they feel that this is better than arbitrarily omitting some of the data that might prove to be pertinent at a later date.

To give one example from material culture of the classification of objects on the basis of cultural function as opposed simply to physical difference, there appear to be two functionally different types of hauling vehicles in Demirciler: (1) log haulers and (2) general-purpose haulers. These are different types of oxcarts. The two types are quite different physically, and no conscientious field worker would fail to describe the difference, because it is so striking. The basis of classification is obvious from the labels given to the classes. The problem is that within class (2) above there are a great variety of physically different carts, but all members of the class serve the same function and are mutually interchangeable so far as the members of the society are concerned.

The discussion of Turkish village culture has been based generally on the above premise, and an attempt was made throughout to discuss categories that were significant within the culture of the village, without making explicit the methodology for categorizing the traits. Interestingly enough the village has been changing rapidly in the past few years, and one very good example of the difference between functionally significant categories and nonsignificant ones can be seen in these changes. Until 1950 the Muhtar was the eldest man in the village—the village was simply a group of kinsmen (because of the strict endogamy), and the Muhtar was the head of this expanded family group. All political power flowed through the family structure, therefore the village did not have a functioning political organization. But with increased communication with the outside world, this kinship system has become less important and in the mid-1950s the head of the kinship group was voted out as Muhtar and

replaced by a younger man. It is highly probable that with increased urbanization the political organization will become much more important and the traditional social organization less so. In discussing the old system a description of
the political organization would have reflected the imposition of what westerners
felt to be an important category of culture on a people for whom this did not
really exist as a part of their culture independent from the social structure.
However, with urbanization (perhaps synonymous with westernization) has
come the development of a Western type of political structure, even within the
village.

The example above covers an entire segment of the culture, and many
other examples could be found in any society. If in a case study of a particular
culture, such as that given above, one does not find a particular thing described,
this may not be an oversight on the part of the field worker, because that particular thing may be subsumed under a different classification in the culture
being studied than it is in the culture of the reader, or perhaps absent in that
culture entirely. This is not to say that every anthropologist describes everything
that he sees objectively and completely. Anthropologists are human, and no
matter how hard one may try, one's own culture creeps into the description.
Further, one always asks himself questions, when reading a cultural description,
for which the author does not provide any answer. This is inescapable, as a
culture is an enormous monster that grows and changes before the very eyes of
the anthropologist as he attempts to describe it. There are always limitations on
his time, interest, and abilities in addition to the enormity of the task.

Looking back for a moment at our brief study of a Turkish village, there
are many things left unsaid about the culture. First, there are odd facts that
cannot be worked easily into any sort of organized description. Sometimes these
fit neatly into place when more field work has been done, but sometimes they
do not. An example of such a fact is the curious bit of information that one of
the elder villagers owns a truck that hauls food products between Adana and
Konya. How did he get this vehicle? How long has he had it? Has anyone else
in the village ever owned one such as this before? What effect does this have
on his situation in the village so far as status, wealth, and so on are concerned?
I simply did not get around to collecting the information with which to answer
all these questions. Even when such information has been gathered, it frequently must be left out of a description because of space limitations in publica-
tions. Perhaps this is a significant weakness, because it is possible that information
of this nature may be just the type that will shed light on more widespread
cultural phenomena.

Second, there are many things about which one either cannot or simply
does not gather information. A good example of this in Demirciler were birth
customs. Since most of my informants were male and knew very little about
such things, it was not possible to elicit such information. Further, because of
the sharp separation between the sexes, it was not possible for me to elicit much
from the women themselves on this subject. One is further plagued by his own
special interests that lead him to explore certain aspects of the culture while
neglecting others. There are also such chance factors as whether there happens

to be a birth, marriage, or death in the village while you are there. If so, well and good; if not, you may be unwilling to simply take the word of your informants without having an opportunity to check the elicited information against observable behavior, and as a result certain things may be omitted from a description. Finally, each reader will have different questions, such as what would happen if someone plowed up a field in the communally-held pasture land. I do not know the answer to such a question, and I doubt if the villagers could answer it either. Besides this, it is impossible for the field worker to anticipate all such questions, so he goes about his business as methodically as possible in terms of his own predilictions and chance circumstances.

Last of all, there are the differences in classification mentioned above. One sometimes attempts to ignore other types of omissions as they could be interpreted by other scholars as sloppy field work, but all of these are inherent in being the human product of a particular culture. This statement is made explicit here only because so many beginning students in anthropology seem to assume that culture is a neatly defined little system and that the anthropologist absorbs this system after a few months residence in the society, and that he has all the answers to any questions about the culture.

Cultures are systems, but they appear to be anything but simple or neat. Depending on one's theoretical inclination, culture can be viewed in many ways, but I consider it to be a system of systems, the functioning of all of which affect the functioning of the other systems, and any alteration of one part causes readjustments in the other parts. Further, cultures are dynamic entities that change, sometimes remarkably fast and at other times hardly at all. These entities can be treated almost as if they have a life of their own, independent of the members of the society, but one must always keep in mind that this is not really the case. Culture exists only in the minds of the members of the society; it is not an object out in space.

Thus any description of a complete culture is by definition impossible, because one would have to describe it forever, with all of the minute variations encountered. Therefore, what one attempts to do is describe the basic components of each of the major subsystems within the culture. If I have succeeded in giving the reader empathy for the basic cultural values of the Turkish villager and an objective understanding of his environment and the pattern of his way of life, I shall have accomplished about all one can hope to do in any book.

Suggested Readings

COON, CARLETON, *Caravan: The Story of the Middle East,* 2d ed. New York: Holt, Rinehart and Winston, Inc., 1958.

This volume is an excellent introduction to the Middle East as a whole. A great deal of the material does not concern itself with Turkey directly, but much of what is said is also true for Anatolia.

LERNER, DANIEL, *The Passing of Traditional Society.* New York: The Free Press of Glencoe, 1958.

A report of a rather extensive study of culture change in the Middle East. Data are presented to document the increase in communication within the area, and an attempt is made to correlate this with the speed of culture change. The village of Balgat, Turkey, is described in some detail as it was in 1949 when first visited and as it was when revisited in 1954. Balgat is near Ankara and changes began to occur earlier and perhaps at a greater speed there than in most of Anatolia.

MAKAL, MAHMOUD, *A Village in Anatolia.* London: Vallentine Press, 1954.

A story of a young Turk born in a village (Demirci, *not* Demirciler, about 80 kilometers southeast of Kaman) and educated in the Irviz Village Institute. As an adult he was sent by the Ministry of Education to the village of Nürgüz (near his birthplace) to bring the message of modernization to the peasants. It documents his tribulations, frustrations, and even anger at his own people because of their tenacity in clinging to the old ways. It is not an organized presentation of village life, but it gives interesting glimpses of Anatolian villages as seen from within by a Turk who is dedicated to the revolution of Mustafa Kemal Atatürk. The author spent many months in jail for writing the book under the Menderes government.

MANTRAN, ROBERT, *Turkey.* Paris: Hachette World Albums, 1955.

An excellent picture presentation of Turkish life and the country side, along with historical monuments.

ORGA, IRFAN, *Portrait of a Turkish Family.* New York: The Macmillan Company, 1950.

A good picture of the life of one Turkish family between the two world wars. This is a very human story and interesting to read.